© Sue Owe

D0527818

ISBN 0-9524

All rights reserved. No part of this publication may be reproduced or transmitted, in any form or by any means, electronic or mechanical, including photocopy, recording or any information storage and retrieval system, without permission in writing from the publisher

Published in the United Kingdom by:

Destiny Ministries
Destiny Church
1120 Pollokshaws Road
Shawlands, Glasgow
G41 3QP

Tel: +44 (0)141 616 6777
Fax: +44 (0)141 616 6300
E-mail: publishing@destinyministries.org.uk

All scripture quotations, unless otherwise indicated, are taken from the Amplified Bible, Copyright © 1954, 1958, 1962, 1964, 1965, 1987 by the Lockman Foundation. Used by permission.

Scripture quotations marked (NIV) are taken from the HOLY BIBLE, NEW INTERNATIONAL VERSION. NIV®. Copyright © 1973, 1978, 1984 by International Bible Society. Used by permission of Zondervan. All rights reserved. Scripture quotations marked (NKJV) are taken from the New King James Version. Copyright © 1982 by Thomas Nelson, Inc. Used by permission. All rights reserved. Scripture quotations marked (NASB) are taken from the New American Standard Bible®, copyright© The Lockman Foundation 1960, 1962, 1963, 1968, 1971, 1972, 1973, 1975, 1977, 1995. Used by Permission. Scripture quotations marked (RSV) are from The Revised Standard Version of the Bible copyright © 1946, 1952 and 1971 by the Division of Christian Education of the National Council of Churches in the USA. Used by permission. All Rights Reserved.

Printing by Summit Media & Print 0845 130 4678

Acknowledgements

My thanks to
Lydia Spicer for her faithful
proof-reading, enthusiasm
and encouragement.

Dedication

To Andrew, my husband,
and Joshua, Daniel, Robert,
Gareth and Simeon our sons,
in this awesome journey.
To Molly, my mum.
I love you all.

To Destiny Church,
this mighty house full of
bravehearts who never settle
for less than God intended.

IS GOD THERE? YOU BET!

INTRODUCTION

Hey there, are you on a journey? How is it going? Is your life hectic, great, tough or plain boring? God wants to share it with you. Have you been looking for Him, because he wants to be found! I don't know what got you to where you are today. Perhaps you ventured through fortune telling, various philosophies or other more religious routes as your journey progressed. We all start somewhere in our quest to find out if there is a God, or if someone like Him could possibly exist.

Please let me tell you that knowing about Him is completely different to actually knowing Him. Being able to hear His voice and share everyday life with Him is the most amazing adventure you could ever dare to embark upon. What's more exciting is that He gives an open invitation to whoever will respond. I certainly did respond. Just look at what happened in my life and see how awesome He is. Quickly check out one of the stories in the book. I dare you to! Believe me, it's all true!

My story began when I was young. I was at school when I first met people who spoke of knowing Jesus who could be my friend forever. They seemed to be different, really peaceful and not stressed out! Yet they were connected to life in a real way. I wondered if it was real and if I could have this life for myself. I wove my way through my childhood and early teenage years with lots of questions and unanswered longings. No one in my family was what you'd call looking for God, so I would tag along with friends to any Sunday school that seemed fun at the time. I know now that I was on a mission, a mission to find my own true best friend. We all have a deep need inside of us to find answers to life's challenges, especially the biggest ones of all! Why are we here? Who can we share it with? I began to recognise a gap in my life that nothing seemed to be able to fill. As I spoke with the others in the Scripture Union at school I realised that I must make a SPECIFIC DECISION and THEN ACT ON THAT DECISION for things to be different!

I asked one of the older girls if she would help me to become a Christian, and we prayed together following a gospel outreach film at school. She seemed quite shocked at my enthusiasm and I don't think she had ever prayed with anyone like me before.

I would have prayed with anyone, my heart was set. The sixth former was really just a witness to my encounter with God himself. That mattered to me, because I'd been secretly asking Jesus into my life for weeks and had not known that he'd answered my very first call.

God knows us through and through but something happens inside us when we INVOLVE ANOTHER PERSON in our decision to accept and follow Jesus. The Bible says:

> *'Because if you acknowledge and confess with your lips that Jesus is Lord and in your heart believe (adhere to, trust in, and rely on the truth) that God raised Him from the dead, you will be saved. For with the heart a person believes (adheres to, trusts in, and relies on Christ) and so is justified (declared righteous, acceptable to God), and with the mouth he confesses (declares openly and speaks out freely his faith) and confirms [his] salvation.'* **Romans 10: 9-10**

Jesus died so that we can get near to God and

have a living relationship with Him. We have to let someone know about the choices we have made. THIS IS ONLY THE BEGINNING because just as a newborn baby must not stay in limbo, but grow and mature, so also must we. Growing up as a Christian requires that we go through many purposeful and life-changing decisions. I thank God for all those patient people who answered my questions, and faithfully taught me many of the Bible's truths that I'm now passing on to my children and those I meet.

We cannot waste time being weak and undernourished as Christians in today's world. This generation requires strong, faith-filled, Christ-like and Christ-minded people who will not buckle under the weight or pressure that life places on them.

As you read you'll join me on my journey, as well as hear of the many and very unusual ways in which I've found God to be involved with my life. I've heard His voice and followed His lead into and through some amazing situations. Almighty God has stooped down so close to us and kept me and my family safe. He has healed our bodies and brought relief from tormenting problems. God certainly is alive and very active on planet earth - even on the small patch where you or I live!

Read on and see for yourself. Some of these real life stories may even help you to dare to believe that God is here for you. Do you know that He longs to be invited into your world, and He will answer your cry when you ask Him to take control? However things look right now, He is willing to get involved with your life and has answers that will supernaturally transform your everyday existence.

1. JOSHUA IS HERE

'God chooses what we go through; we choose how we go through it.'[1]

John C Maxwell

I was full term with Samuel, our firstborn son, when everything went still inside me. At the hospital we were told that he'd died, and immediately the doctors began to talk of tests that we would have to undergo once he was born. They wanted to induce the labour but we were not ready to just let go of our baby. Maybe, just maybe, there could be a miracle. We went home and prayed for what seemed like a long five days. We immediately began to ask God for that miracle and also that I would go into labour soon. Some people were fasting and they urgently wanted me to go into labour!

Even as we rushed to hospital on that Tuesday teatime I believed God could give him back and expected to feel a kick. I had waited so long at home that the baby was almost born in the car. He was delivered easily and with little fuss and I remember sensing an awesome wonder at the creation of a new baby.

He looked perfect and I had a peace that was beyond human understanding. A great sense of comfort filled the room, as we knew we must let him go. GOD IS NEVER TAKEN BY SURPRISE AND HE CAN TURN ANY SITUATION AROUND. I didn't ask why this had happened but I did wonder what on earth was this bolt from the blue that had tried to destroy all hope in our lives. It did not make sense and I wanted to see things from God's perspective.

You see, later on God whispered into my heart what the enemy had thought. He thought he could destroy me, and that I would be crushed and disabled forever, unable to fulfil God's mandate and calling because of this huge tragedy and loss. God told me that He had a different plan for my life.

GOD HAS A DIFFERENT PLAN FOR YOUR LIFE.

The medics looked for a reason for Samuel's death, but the tests revealed nothing. As we looked into the possibilities of trying for another child, I knew that my sense of self-worth and value could not be found in motherhood. I learned that lesson there and then! All the usual stages of grief kicked into gear, yet I had God with me. We didn't want to wait long before beginning another pregnancy and three months later I conceived for the second time. The new baby was to be born exactly twelve months after Samuel, just before Christmas!

Scripture tells us that Jesus is to be our all in all. That our joy and strength are found in Him … I began to experience these truths over the next months and they are still alive and established in me today. Psalm 68 tells us:

'Kings of armies flee, they flee, and she who remains at home divides the spoil.'
Psalm 68: 12 (NKJV)

'Blessed be the Lord, Who bears our burdens and carries us day by day …'
Psalm 68: 19

'Your God has commanded your strength; Strengthen O God, what You have done for us.' **Psalm 68: 28 (NKJV)**

'O God, You are more awesome than Your holy places. The God of Israel is He who gives strength and power to His people.'
Psalm 68:35 (NKJV)

God clearly wants to make us strong and fill our lives with good things. Sometimes we have to wait to meet our blessing in our heavenly home, but often we meet it here as we learn to bring heaven to earth.

'Behold, children are a heritage from the Lord, the fruit of the womb a reward.'
Psalms 127: 3 (NIV)

Yes, children are gifts from God and they are a token of His love. Yet LIFE IN HIM is where TRUE PURPOSE can be found. It's not all in our families or our jobs or in how many exams we manage to pass. If everything we live for is to be found in our children, what do we become if, and more likely when, they all leave home? If our whole lives are to be found hidden in our careers, do we cease to function or lose our sense of value if we give up work? I think not, because it is WHO WE ARE IN CHRIST THAT GIVES US OUR IDENTITY, not our qualifications, possessions or achievements. Everything else is a beautiful bonus, and an opportunity to steward the riches of heaven.

I also knew back then that a new baby could not possibly become the substitute for the one who'd been given back into the arms of God. I was totally excited as I thought about our new baby and at the same time was considering what had recently happened in our lives.

Tackling the grief was a journey in itself and a necessary process that one couldn't avoid. Quite soon afterwards I became caught by some difficulties that needed addressing. I knew I could not ignore the problems and I did not want to hide behind a veneer of pretence.

I NEEDED HELP WITH MY THOUGHT LIFE (my mindset).

Something had clearly gone wrong with my perspective on life because my inner world sank. Within a few short months, I needed to be rescued from patterns of negative thinking which, in my depressed state, I allowed to gain a foothold. Twelve weeks into the second pregnancy I painfully and foolishly almost talked myself into another tragedy. I was expecting the worst all the time for what seemed like a long six or seven weeks.

You see, out of concern a friend had said something to me which sounded kind, but caused me to worry. They wanted the doctor to find out what had caused the first pregnancy to fail. The doctor couldn't give an explanation even after all the tests he put us through. It almost totally dissolved away my faith in God for this second pregnancy. Unwittingly, I'd let in this negativity, caused by my friend's love, through a chink in my armour! Love must be tough, and we must guard against the desire to pamper our emotions. I needed to repent (say sorry) and then deliberately change course.

I ASKED GOD ABOUT THE CAUSE OF MY NEGATIVE MINDSET AND HE CLEARLY TOLD ME THAT I'D HEARD WRONG, I'D RECEIVED THE WRONG MESSAGE AND THAT IT WAS DEFINITELY NOT FROM HEAVEN - IT WAS NOT THE EXPRESSION OF HIS HEART FOR ME. The person who loved me projected his concerns and worries onto my life and at first the conversation seemed harmless, yet it ultimately nearly destroyed our future. The Bible tells us that:

> '... *faith comes from hearing the message, and the message is heard through the word of Christ.*'   **Romans 10:17(NIV)**

I needed to get tough in order not to bring calamity back into my life. I asked for forgiveness and for this destructive power to be broken. I CONFESSED MY MISTAKE AS I PRAYED, AND I CUT OFF ITS POWER IN THE NAME OF THE LORD.

I KNEW THAT MY FAITH MUST GROW SO I DID A MAJOR STUDY ON STRENGTH AND JOY FROM THE PASSAGES OF THE BIBLE. I also decided that if I needed medical help for me or our new baby I would go at once and get it, and not simply stay at home hoping the problem would go away.

We were going to be visiting a Christian conference during the summer. I was already five and a half months pregnant with our second baby and I was really unhappy about having to see everyone from my larger world of friends and associates. Life continues and often we're not given time out to get over things - I knew I'd have to tell people that our first baby son had died and now I was expecting our second child. That's not an easy task when everyone is away on a happy family camp and no matter how you try, you can't help but think you're spoiling the fun!

The sense of failure is a very real hurdle to overcome. In the past I've been a very private person and I have always endeavoured to 'have it all together'. Being a leader in the church you're required to be stronger than steel and I know only too well that eyes watch with eager concentration to see how to do this thing called life. You are completely aware of the responsibility you carry because people watch and definitely copy your lifestyle. One thing I've always wanted to be is an inspiration to others to dare to believe that God is for them and that they can more than make it in this Christian life.

What was more important to me though, was the sense of calling on our lives and how much we needed to be strong for the sake of what the Lord had stored up for us to do! We've had many prophecies over our lives that have spoken of trials and things that would cause us to be tested in our loyalty and commitment. After a long time it became very daunting and heavy and I dreaded what might be said next. I began to sense these words were literally creating the things that were being spoken of. I now take a double check on things that are said and sincerely and carefully weigh these words. The Bible says that prophecy is intended to encourage us, build us up and cause us to be wiser in our daily lives.

SO MANY PEOPLE THINK THAT BECAUSE A WORD HAS A 'THUS SAITH THE LORD' WRAPPED AROUND IT THAT IT MUST BE FROM GOD! People can feel like this especially when a word is brought in a large public meeting, but these words must be weighed. If received without question they can alter the whole course of the next ten years for someone!

Tragedy can set people on a course of growth or destruction. Often they either hit the Bible or hit the bottle. I knew that I needed to grow as a woman of resolve and to grow quickly. I needed to get strong, to think the right thoughts which would cause me to speak more positively, and then, finally, I would be able to live in the best of what God had planned.

WITH DIVINE SCHOOLING YOU CAN GROW THAT STRENGTH! WITH GOD IT WILL BE AN AWESOME KIND OF STRENGTH THAT ONLY HE CAN PRODUCE AND ONLY HE CAN RECEIVE THE GLORY FOR.

I searched the Bible for every verse that brought encouragement and talked of joy and faith. I needed to learn so much so quickly, and not in my head only but especially in my heart. It proved to be a life-changing lesson for our whole family.

I went to the Lord himself, often. A one-off encounter was never enough and it became second nature for me to involve God in almost every part of my days and nights. Praying for five minutes in the morning seemed useless and I became dependent on His presence for all of my needs. I had to have peace, quiet and privacy to pour my heart out before him.

Many people book appointments to see their GP or counsellor but I knew where to get continual and lasting help. He is only a whisper away. Scripture says that we're to cast our burden on the Lord and I believe that when I come to Him I cannot bring something He doesn't already know about and have an answer for.

> *'Casting all your care upon Him, for He cares for you.'* **1 Peter 5:7 (NKJV)**

I gave all of my heartache to God and talked to Him about the disappointments and the grief. People who are hurting are nearer to God than they know, because His basic nature is to counsel and comfort, whoever they are!

I remember wanting to meet God up close so that I could talk to Him about the thing that had hit us so unexpectedly. I'd cried and prayed often as you can imagine, but one particular night I had a special encounter with Him. I poured everything out in English and also in tongues (my heavenly language), until there was nothing left. Once I was empty I began to ask the Lord to fill me again with His healing love, and He did - in an unforgettable way.

I just began to sing and thank Him for His wonderful love and presence. It was awesome to know that God was aware of me and that He was with me in it all. New songs of adoration began to flow. God gave me more than I'd bargained for. Where there had been confusion I now had peace and where there had been disappointment there was hope. What is more, where I had felt a deep sense of failure, the promise of purpose for my future was very real to me. At the same time the overwhelmed and daunted feeling I'd had was replaced by a renewed strength. All of this came to me because of my relationship with Jesus Christ.

Before conceiving Samuel we had tried to start a family for almost a year and the wait had seemed endless to me at the time. When the baby was due to be born, and just the night before he went still, Andrew read the Biblical story of Hannah and Samuel out loud and it was a very special moment for me. Hannah, in the first chapter of 1 Samuel, had asked the Lord for a child, because she hadn't yet conceived. She did fall pregnant, gave birth to Samuel and then gave her son to the Lord as she'd promised months before. I remember facing the same challenge, just days later! Then she went on to have five more children! This sounds familiar!

Still at this point in my journey, I was facing my weakness and failure, and I had decided to change course and to turn things around.

> 'So do not fear, for I am with you; do not be dismayed, for I am your God. I will strengthen you and help you; I will uphold you with my righteous right hand.'
>
> **Isaiah 41:10 (NIV)**

> 'O God, you are more awesome than your holy places. The God of Israel is He who gives strength and power to His people ...'
>
> **Psalms 68:35 (NKJV)**

I sure was desperate for this kind of input right then. I also needed the honest comfort of dear friends who would talk God's talk to me. Sympathy would have touched my soul but it would have changed nothing in my spirit. As a Christian woman, I have decided to be LED BY THE HOLY SPIRIT. He is my helper, my coach and my mentor. He is the one who helps to make my spirit (my inner being, or my heart) strong.

I CAN KNOW OF THE HOLY SPIRIT OR I CAN CHOOSE TO KNOW HIM - THERE IS A DIFFERENCE! I know of many celebrities but just because they're on TV each day it doesn't mean that I know them personally. I remember hearing about the Holy Spirit in my teenage years and desperately wanted to meet Him. Once we'd been introduced though, it was my responsibility to keep this new friendship alive.

It's a relationship that I need to have, to move forward and grow as a Christian. If I leave Him out, I'm missing much of the wisdom, comfort and training for life that is necessary for me to be a winner! I know that I have to cultivate this friendship and keep it strong, by putting time in and making it a priority. I decided to avoid the soaps on TV as they so often contain enough sorrow and fear to last a lifetime. These do not carry God's perspective into a Christian's life, as entertaining as many people think they are!

It was also unbelievable just how many documentaries and newspaper articles there were on stillbirths at that time. I could have become totally engrossed in it all, especially in a quest to understand more and find a reason for our tragedy. The friend whose comments had affected me so much had actually advised us to do just that. I KNEW FOR ME THAT WAS NOT THE WAY FORWARD on this occasion! I knew I must trust the Lord and recognise that my strength would come by filling myself with God's powerful life-bringing word.

The key verse in the Bible is found in the book of Psalms:

'It is better to trust and take refuge in the Lord than to put confidence in man. It is better to trust and take refuge in the Lord than to put confidence in princes.'
Psalms 118:8-9

God was telling me that I had to trust Him and not go on some wild-goose chase to satisfy my unanswered questions. Experts are everywhere, and we can choose to listen, yet the word of God says that it is BETTER to trust in the Lord than to trust in men. The Bible also says that it is BETTER to trust in the Lord than to put our trust in princes. We are not told not to listen, or not to trust them. We are told that IT'S BETTER TO TRUST IN THE LORD.

It is a good idea to be careful if you're facing financial problems or relationship difficulties in your life. To listen to someone's advice is one thing, but to put your total confidence in what they say is taking things to another level. 'You become what you take in' may be true of foodstuffs for your body, but it also applies to the head knowledge and advice all around you. You are changed by what you unwittingly and/or unwisely consume.

> *'... It has been written, Man shall not live and be upheld and sustained by bread alone, but by every word that comes forth from the mouth of God.'* **Matthew 4:4**

To a Christian the word of God (the Bible) is literally their bread. It's the thing that gives us strength and stamina for the next step or decision. Let's make sure that what we get is good and fresh, and that we eat it every day!

We need a relevant word that is alive for today's challenge, just as much as we need new food for every new day. First we must admit our concern and take a long hard look at the challenge. Then we need to submit the situation to God for His Fatherly advice. When we invite His comment and wisdom we must go to the Bible and ask Him to lead us clearly. God responds by highlighting particular truths that help in our situation. Often there is a word to encourage and strengthen. Sometimes it can be a word of warning and we must pray expectantly believing that He will help us.

Christians love to be spoon fed, but we need to learn to get the goodness of the word of God for ourselves. There are starving Christians everywhere but God is also building up houses of bread where the NOW word of the Lord is spoken in a clear and understandable way. These are places where the relevant message for today's generation is being taught regularly, so that weakness, misunderstanding and confusion become a thing of the past.

It is not enough to go to a church only because the music is good or the teaching feeds your intellectual mind. The word of God in all its power must be taught, with signs and wonders following. We need a word from heaven, which teaches biblical truth that can connect with the challenges that people face in this day and age.

During that season over eighteen years ago I also endeavoured to keep away from negative and worrying newspaper and magazine articles. I literally cocooned myself for weeks as I purposefully aimed my whole life at becoming strong and well-disciplined in my thought life. It was a journey that I believe was lifesaving.

For a marathon an athlete will think nothing of preparing his body and mind, because he wants to win. This was one marathon that I also wanted to win. The sense of failure and shame can be very real as one takes the journey through grief. I did not want to face it again!

For many weeks there was a lot of investment going into my spiritual life, and it proved to be very valuable indeed. I searched the Bible for stories of hope, I checked through many of the promises to Christian people that are written there. I prayed before I read anything, that God would help me to find what I needed for the day. I avoided people who might be overly worried for me and the baby so that they couldn't project their fear onto us. I prayed in tongues a lot!

The challenge was still ahead at that time and ALL THE TRAINING I'D BEEN THROUGH WAS ABOUT TO BE TESTED!

About 28 weeks into my second pregnancy I realised the baby was quiet, I didn't feel right. I decided that rather than stay at home and get worried I would simply have a check up at the doctor's, then carry on with my day. It wasn't quite as simple as I'd hoped. My husband, Andrew dropped me off at the doctor's surgery so that he could take care of some things and we had arranged to meet outside in about an hour. We need to know at all times that we are never alone and that our loving heavenly Father is by our side in all situations. He is only a breath away.

When the doctor felt my huge pregnant tummy I could see that he was a little concerned. I told him that the baby had not been kicking for quite a long time and that I'd rather visit him for a quick check-up, than stay at home to think on it.

He began the usual round of examinations as most ladies who have had children will remember! He seemed to be taking quite a long time to find what he was looking for right then. At first he just asked me to turn a little, he examined me again and then I noticed he was flushed.

On listening in for the baby's heartbeat his face began to show panic and he started to hyperventilate and had to sit down. He also was trying to see if he could feel any of the baby's movements. I realised he was very worried but that he did not want to alarm me.

'Please go to the hospital Mrs Owen', he quietly said, as he wrote a note for the staff there. I saw what he had written and I understood the doctors' abbreviations. He had put NFMF (no foetal movement felt), and NFHH (no foetal heartbeat heard). In layman's terms this basically means that he thought this baby had died. The baby was not moving and the doctor could not find the heartbeat!

I KNEW THERE AND THEN THAT I HAD A CHOICE TO MAKE!

I could simply fall on my face and dissolve into hysterics, or else stir up that faith I'd been growing, and get before God Himself, in the street. I quietly got dressed to go outside and walked down the path, knowing that Andrew was not expecting this news and that I'd better be ready for him too.

I SET TO (that's my way of saying I gathered my best thoughts), and REMINDED GOD OF ALL THE PROMISES THAT I HAD FOUND. I'D BEEN DELIBERATELY SEARCHING THEM OUT IN MY HANDBOOK FOR LIFE, MY BIBLE. I had to forcefully stir up my spirit and then I called to my memory the truths I'd been discovering.

Once more I proclaimed God's strength over this child. I sang adoration and power to the King of Kings over this child. I KNOW THAT WHEN RAW PRAISE HITS THE HEAVENS THAT GOD GETS INVOLVED AND BRINGS HIS STRENGTH INTO THE SITUATION.

Something snapped in my spirit as I violently declared this baby was mine to keep. There were very few people around and I prayed forcefully that this baby was not for the taking, and I would accept nothing less than a healthy bouncing child. The boy or girl question never came into it as you can imagine!

I had to get it together for when Andrew came back as I didn't want him to panic! I just said we needed a little check up and that it would be

OK! A classic understatement! At the mention of hospital he drove so fast I nearly gave birth in the passenger seat! On reading the doctor's letter the staff took me to a side room. It all seemed so familiar and brought back memories of when I'd been there almost one year before.

Here I was again holding my breath and watching my mouth. In these tense moments it is too easy sometimes to blurt out an irrational fear or a negative comment. I knew that as I'd confessed health and strength into this tiny body during those earlier months of development, something had been activated.

I WAS NOT GOING TO THROW IT ALL AWAY NOW. If I had done I would have opened the door for all sorts of destructive things to happen. The baby was totally quiet and not moving at all. By this time he had been still for a number of hours, even though the doctor and I had been pummelling my tummy to try to feel some movement.

However, once the big strap was around my tummy the nurse found our sleeping son rolled into a tight curl, still quite motionless but VERY MUCH ALIVE! I knew I had to walk by faith and not by sight on this occasion and I could have buckled under what I felt my body AND THE DOCTOR'S NOTE were telling me. Even what we see with our own eyes can have an adverse effect on us as we face things. We must never step into defeat before the light of God's word has been shone on the situation. DON'T BELIEVE YOUR BODY. DON'T BELIEVE WHAT YOU SEE, HEAR, IMAGINE OR FEEL.

'For we walk by faith, not by sight.'
2 Corinthians 5: 7(NKJV)

So many Christians shadow box because they feel caught by the 'faith' message which seems to have implied you're a failure if you admit that you are in difficulty or that you are concerned about something. They stay at home in isolation or embark on a battle that might not even be theirs to engage in.

We need to know who or what our enemy is so that we can face him or it without fear. I am not a doctor and had no way of knowing that the baby was OK, I could have stayed at home paralysed with worry, not daring to get checked out. I could have spent hours shadow boxing with scriptures and faith-stirring songs and done the whole deal alone.

Going to the hospital meant that if the baby needed to be born there and then, I'd have been ready too. His safety was the most important thing to me, but I think God had my spiritual growth on His mind. I don't have time to waste and once I know the score, I can then tackle things head on.

We are to live by faith and that means going into the secret place to find a word from heaven that will fuel our spirit and strengthen our will to fight. We're allowed to furnish it with emotion and passion and then let rip at the adversary. His intention is to devour us, kill whatever he can and steal everything in the process.

GOD'S INTENTION IS QUITE THE OPPOSITE AND HIS LOVE FOR US IS ENORMOUS! We have to lean all over Him and tell him how desperate we are for His truth and His intervention. God's plans for us are good.

'They overcame him by the blood of the Lamb and by the word of their testimony; They did not love their lives so much as to shrink from death.' **Revelation 12: 11 (NIV)**

When we testify to His almighty power and speak of His strength, majesty and rule, and then pray concerning the blood of Jesus, we are actually reminding the Father of His covenant with us. We come not with a boldness concerning who we are but with the authority of WHAT CHRIST HAS DONE. We can be so changeable and subject to moods but what Christ has done can never be altered, bettered or rendered powerless.

What Jesus did bought us our relationship with the Father and it's a finished and accomplished work. We totally belong to Him. He approached us first and is delighted that we're His children. He cannot resist it when we tell Him who He is, and that we belong to Him. We're His responsibility because we've been purchased by Jesus' blood that was shed on the cross. The moment we are born again, God in heaven becomes a brand new daddy and He takes his fathering seriously!

BIG DADDY SHOWS UP WHEN HE HEARS HIS DAUGHTERS WAILING.

Josh is 18 years old now and he totally loves and lives for God and music. He is tall, dark and handsome and still loves his sleep! He is completely gorgeous - and I know I'm biased!

'It's not whether you get knocked down, it's whether you get up.'[2] **Vince Lombardi**

KEY POINTS TO REMEMBER.

1. Do not always believe what your body wants to tell you.

2. Do not always take as your future what the expert has said to you.

3. Believe the word that God has made to live in your heart and get strength from it to hold you up when you feel like crumbling.

4. When you need confidence, search for it and find it in the Bible not a magazine or the latest TV programme. Decide to keep away from the things and the people that might confuse you or cause you to worry.

5. When you feel alone in your battle know that God will never leave you.

6. Get into a church that honours God first and that feeds the people the truth of the Bible in life. Lives will depend on it!

2. HOUSE MOVE (1)

> '*In The middle of difficulty lies opportunity.*'[3]   **Albert Einstein**

We knew it was the right thing to move to Scotland in the late 1980's. We needed to sell our house and bring our family to Glasgow as soon and as easily as possible. We had a dream to pioneer and bring together a vibrant church of people who loved God and would serve Him with all their energy - a people who lived for Him, not just sang to Him on a Sunday! We began to work towards making this dream a reality. During the following months Andrew made frequent trips to Scotland to begin the work, settle the people who were pioneering with us and to search for a new home for us.

I was grounded for much of the autumn because by then we had three little boys and they took it in turns to have chickenpox. It seemed to take a long few weeks to clear up. There were lots of things to do as I prepared for us to relocate. There was quite a lot of hassle and we had a few difficulties to deal with along the way. We advertised our home with the agents and found that our phone number was misprinted in the newspaper. That was the first advertisement and it just didn't work. We placed another advert in the paper which was accurate this time.

HOWEVER AN HOUR BEFORE PEOPLE WERE COMING TO VIEW WE REALISED THERE WAS A FAULT IN THE ELECTRICITY SUPPLY. Usually everything worked fine in the house and I desperately needed to vacuum the place having the three boys under five! Andrew was away and the viewers were due to arrive and I felt so concerned that the place needed to look good.

What a joy! The children and I prayed and the power came on just in time!

Everything seemed to be coming together well, but progress is not without its struggles. To be born, a baby has to push through some tight spots, and to emerge the butterfly has to fight its way out of the chrysalis - and be changed beyond recognition in the process! Christianity is not a cop out or a lifestyle for weak, spineless people. In fact, some of the most influential people I know are CHRISTIANS WHO, AGAINST ALL ODDS, HAVE SIMPLY DECIDED NOT TO QUIT.

It's a lifestyle of strategy, power and sheer guts as we go forward to be what and where God wants us to be.

> *'Looking away [from all that will distract] to Jesus, Who is the Leader and the Source of our faith [giving the first incentive for our belief] and is also it's Finisher [bringing it to maturity and perfection]. He, for the joy [of obtaining the prize] that was set before Him, endured the cross, despising and ignoring the shame, and is now seated at the right hand of the throne of God.'*
> **Hebrews 12:2**

We have never had to face that challenge, yet His determination and endurance speak to us today. JESUS FOCUSED all of His strength on getting to the cross and beyond. He agreed with the Father and the Holy Spirit that He should come to earth and put down His heavenly comforts for a while.

HE WAS NOT OUT ON A SUNDAY AFTERNOON PICNIC WHEN HE OBEYED AND CAME HERE SO THAT WE COULD

BE RESCUED FROM THE CLUTCHES OF THE DEVIL!

Often we learn as we go along, and one of the main lessons is that the one who gives in is never going to see the prize. We have to continue to the end and be in on the action through the whole course of events, praying as we go forward. Life is full of stuff to deal with and it's not just the spiritual detail that God has an answer for. He wants to be included in the ordinary things that we have to face.

> *'Commit your way to the Lord [roll and repose each care of your load on Him]; trust (lean on, rely on, and be confident) also in Him, and He will bring it to pass.'*
> **Psalms 37:5**

A few weeks later we thought we'd sold to a lady. She was very specific in her acceptance of the house and said that she would speak to her lawyers in the near future. It seemed a bit odd but she went on holiday for three weeks and we waited for lawyers' papers. Nothing came even after numerous phone calls. SHE HAD CHANGED HER MIND and didn't like to disappoint us, and so we didn't know until well into the winter that we must start the whole process again.

I remember telling the mums at the school gate that we'd be gone by Christmas and we were already into November at that stage. Every one of the people I spoke to about it said that we'd missed the moment now. It was winter and people don't move house in winter, and furthermore the housing market was falling rapidly into recession. I had a decision to make again, and the Holy Spirit helped me by reminding me to praise God over and above my circumstances. I remember having been taught about the power of praise and worship as a teenager. I would often lift my voice and heart higher than the circumstances by singing my way into His presence. PROCLAIMIMG GOD'S MAJESTY IS NOT AN EMOTIONAL EXERCISE BUT A SPIRITUAL STRATEGY that has been given to us to change situations.

When we sing or shout adoration to the Lord with confessions of His power, strength and majesty, something happens in the spiritual realm. We remind ourselves of how awesome He is, we remind the enemy of Who is stacked against him, and of Who it is that is on our side. We especially remind the Lord of how much we are counting on Him to wield His power. He can't resist a good fight on behalf of His believing children.

> *'Put Me in remembrance; Let us contend together; State your case, that you may be acquitted (justified).'*
> **Isaiah 43:26 (NKJV, brackets mine)**

> *'For the eyes of the LORD run to and fro throughout the whole earth, to show Himself strong on behalf of those whose heart is loyal to Him ...'*
> **2 Chronicles 16:9 (NKJV)**

HE REMEMBERS HIS PATERNAL ROLE TOWARDS US. AT THE MOMENT WE'RE BORN AGAIN WE BECOME HIS CHILDREN AND HE BECOMES A DADDY ALL OVER AGAIN. Adam threw away this close relationship and friendship with God in the beginning of time. Yet God's hope and intention has never changed. He wants a huge family and we can be part of it.

I know that He is great and He is more than able to handle anything that affects or hinders me. He never forgets or changes His mind. He never forgets to be daddy or becomes bored with His responsibilities like some earthly dads can do. He is bigger than our humanity and still shows grace to us when we stand in our human weakness.

We can read of the champions of faith in Hebrews:

'Who by [the help of] faith subdued kingdoms, administered justice, obtained promised blessings, closed the mouths of lions, Extinguished the power of raging fire, escaped the devourings of the sword, out of frailty and weakness won strength and became stalwart, even mighty and resistless in battle, routing alien hosts.'
Hebrews 11:3-34

God wants to do spectacular things through ordinary people like you and I. Christ Jesus cannot turn and cast a shadow.

'Every good gift and every perfect (free, large, full) gift is from above; it comes down from the Father of all [that gives] light, in [the shining of] Whom there can be no variation [rising or setting] or shadow cast by His turning [as in an eclipse].
James 1:17

When it comes to God's love, there is never a variation because He does not play games or hide from us. Isn't it wonderful! Nothing can come in between that love either which is a powerful truth!

'For I am persuaded beyond doubt (am sure) that neither death nor life, nor angels nor principalities, nor things impending and threatening nor things to come, nor powers,

[39]Nor height nor depth, nor anything else in all creation will be able to separate us from the love of God which is in Christ Jesus our Lord.'   **Romans 8:38-39**

I would fill the house with the best Christian music I could find, and have lyrics of faith echoing around the walls. I now know more than ever that when we lift the name of Jesus high over our situations the spotlight of our attention shifts from the problem, and instead it begins to illuminate the fact that He's the answer. It changes that old mindset within us, which then alters the way we pray and talk about all that is happening around.

It's not enough to pray and then go away and grumble or talk doubt. Neither can we exalt God over our need and then exalt the need again by agreeing with others that the situation is out of hand or too big to deal with.

God had told me He would teach me how to wage war when I was in my middle twenties and I remember feeling excited. I thought that somehow this was going to be quite glamorous. How wrong I was! Wearing a Khaki uniform wasn't what I'd anticipated or looked forward to as a young woman. After many weeks of praising and praying every moment of every day, I asked for a break. Who wouldn't? It all seemed too intense and I thought God was expecting too much of me! SURELY GOD DIDN'T THINK I COULD KEEP GOING LIKE THIS? Wasn't it all a bit fanatical?

We only needed to sell a house but the battle we were having seemed ridiculous – it was like a brick wall was in the way. Something was clearly trying to stop us from relocating. I realised this move was far more important than we'd first thought. Then I had a little insight and a revelation! God clearly told me that if a soldier sat on the battlefield waiting for some light refreshments, the enemy would not quickly become the waiter! Over the years our enemies have changed; that was thirteen years ago!

I took the point and continued to press through. I prayed and kept on singing praise for the answer to come, in every way I knew how. I DETERMINED TO CONTINUE RAISING MY HEAD ABOVE TIREDNESS AND DISCOURAGEMENT.

Andrew was away for over half of every week and I really wanted us to be able to work together and see things take shape.

The Bible says in Psalms 37: 22

> *'For such as are blessed of God shall [in the end] inherit the earth ...'* **Psalms 37:22**

I often told the Lord that we were moving to Scotland to work with and for Him and that we would be going to the North whether we sold the house or not. I asked Him WHERE WOULD THE GLORY BE FOR HIM, THOUGH, IF THE HOUSE WENT TO RUINS AFTER WE'D LEFT? The decision had clearly been made and agreed upon. We would not be changing our minds if the house did not sell! Yet I would explain that He wouldn't get the glory, if our house became empty and was left to go derelict. I don't think He needed me to help Him understand the situation, but I did it anyway! What kind of a testimony to His provision and our confession of faith was that going to be? I know He's an economical and wise God and waste is not a part of His agenda. I just deeply desire that He has an opportunity to reveal His power through our lives and this includes our financial and business dealings.

Having missed one buyer I looked for other keys to unlock the potency of overcoming prayer and quite soon after that I can only say I had a vision.

I WAS UPSTAIRS IN THE BACK BEDROOM (God does not just speak to His people when they're at church), when I saw feathers flying under our willow tree. It was a buzzard that was devouring a small bird. Having never seen anything like that before I called one of the boys to come and see it. He was fascinated with nature, even as a young boy, and he asked if we could go to take a closer look. Of course the buzzard flew away as we went outside and walked towards it. In fact it seemed to simply disappear before our eyes.

What was more surprising to me however was the fact that there was not one feather to be seen anywhere, nor were there any little signs that there had just been a 'scene' on the grass. I puzzled over it for a couple of days because I knew there must be a lesson in there somewhere. I recall asking God to explain to me about what I'd seen and he reminded me of this scripture:

> *'So be subject to God. Resist the devil [stand firm against him], and he will flee from you.'* **James 4:7**

All the way through I had been praying prayers this way! I'd been doing this as I'd fervently called for answers to come to our situation.

In the scriptures Jesus said:

'The thief comes only in order to steal and kill and destroy. I came that they may have and enjoy life, and have it in abundance (to the full, till it overflows). **John 10:10**

I remembered also, however, that as the devil comes as a preying thief, he also has a very keen hunting mentality. This means that he does not like to let go of spoil gained. Another verse to qualify this is:

'Be well balanced (temperate, sober of mind), vigilant and cautious at all times; for that enemy of yours, the devil, roams around like a lion roaring [in fierce hunger], seeking someone to seize upon and devour.' **1 Peter 5:8**

In the unusual vision that took place in my garden it was clear that the bird had kept hold of its lunch. It couldn't eat at the scene of the crime so it decided to have a carry-out! Even in fear and flight there was a strong possessive streak which meant that the bird would not let go of its catch. That incident dramatically changed my prayer language! I then began to pray in a new way and use different terminology.

I always pray and confess that our lives are totally submitted to God's plan. We live for no other purpose. Yet before praying for the enemy to flee, I first want to see that his hands are emptied of our stuff!

I realise that as Christians we often resist the enemy but he has been running away and escaping with our belongings. At least he could take something back in the form of a victory then. Not a good conclusion if you're the one being robbed! I BEGAN TO PRAY THAT HE WOULD FIRST BE DISARMED BEFORE

HE HAD TO FLEE. Also, that he could take nothing of ours with him as he went. He must go to report total defeat.

Not one piece of my deliverance or reward was to be released to him. He must be totally ransacked before he left. I was becoming more desperate for an answer as I thought of holding on to our peace and securing a total victory in the situation. I felt this was important if God was going to look good through it.

I know God doesn't need our help, but the Bible says:

> '…With men this is impossible, but all things are possible with God.'
> **Matthew 19:26**

The above statement does not say 'for God', it says 'with God', which means there's a partnership involved! He wants to work with us, we must comply with Him. JOKINGLY I SAID THAT WHAT WE NEEDED WAS AN IMPATIENT PERSON WHO DIDN'T HAVE A PROPERTY TO SELL AND WHO WOULDN'T NEED TO SECURE A MORTGAGE EITHER.

The following day the phone rang and I ushered the boys into the kitchen with me as I handed the phone to Andrew. I know he's very persuasive and sure enough this person who wanted to buy an old fashioned property with character was about to visit us the following day in our modern home! We had put character into it however; and he had the skill to bring her through the doors.

The family arrived to take a look at our house, and it was my job again to show them around. Andrew was away to work in Scotland for the weekend. Even as they took their time to view I had a sense of excitement welling up in my heart. Some of the children were choosing their bedrooms. The others were talking about where they'd put their furniture. Things looked promising!

I remembered the songs of victory I'd sung with the boys during those long months of waiting. I thought about the scene of the buzzard in the garden that had prompted me to pray in a fresh and strategic way.

THE DEVIL IS A THIEF AND HE WAS ALWAYS TRYING TO TAKE THINGS FROM US. If it wasn't our health, it was our money or our freedom. He'd already taken one potential buyer from me. Now I was on the warpath and I knew that this was my buyer! I was holding on real tight this time.

I asked if they had sold their home to hear that they were renting a place. THAT MEANT THAT THEY DIDN'T HAVE ONE TO SELL, and with all those time-consuming details dealt with it would be quicker. THEY ASKED ME HOW SOON WE COULD MOVE, as if they were in a hurry to get settled! Finally, without any enquiry from me, they also told me that they would buy the place with the help of a business partner and WOULD NOT HAVE TO NEGOTIATE FOR A MORTGAGE. THIS WAS IT! We had taken out a bridging loan, having already signed the papers to buy our new house in Scotland and we were not going to let things drift for long. The first week of December was upon us and there was a lot of work to do for us to be able to relocate by Christmas.

During the next two weeks I had to move fast. Andrew had a dream about the selling of the house the night before we were due to leave England. In it he was told 'you've been to the courts and won!', and God told him that we would grow a large church of thousands.

The following day there was hassle over some parts of the contract, the buyers were actually trying to add some things to it that we'd not agreed on before. They actually said they'd back out of the deal if we didn't comply and change things. Because of the dream we knew we need not give ground and could confidently trust God to see us through!

We didn't have to lose anything and the people bought the house. It turned out to be only twenty-one days from the day they first telephoned us, until the day they moved their furniture in. I packed as speedily as I could, and we moved to Scotland four days before Christmas in 1989.

God loves to partner with us as we negotiate life and work towards the plans He has for us. It is truly amazing to watch how He is passionate for His glory and how He will jealously preserve it. We would have moved anyway. We knew for sure that it was His decision that we should be here, but not at a price dictated to us by the enemy.

I could not see how a move that left a property to go to ruin or to become run down, would be economical or glorifying to Him. I had prayed along those lines. God moved mightily by making possible what, as the house market was dying, we were told just should not happen.

The house we came to was also a miracle. Andrew had seen it months before and fallen for its high ceilings and beautiful woodwork. Because I was often at home in England with the children I could only view it on the day that all the offers were going in for it. At this point we were unable to bid on it. We scoured the papers and a few weeks later that same property was re-advertised at a better price. The previous sale had fallen through, which should not be possible according to Scottish law.

When we put our offer in we openly told the sellers that we would not let them down. This secured the purchase for us at a cheaper price. Peace of mind was really important for the elderly owners who were heading for a retirement flat. They were also doing their best to avoid a bridging-loan, which they didn't want at their stage in life.

To move to another nation and a city we didn't know, was quite a trip with three young children. For every new move there needs to be a word of comfort and faith because when the trial comes along it's the only thing that can hold you. With God we can do anything and His word sustained me:

'For you shall go out [from the spiritual exile caused by sin and evil into the homeland] with joy and be led forth [by your Leader, the Lord Himself, and His word] with peace; the mountains and the hills shall break forth before you into singing, and all the trees of the field shall clap their hands.' **Isaiah 55: 12**

'Let the whole earth His power confess.' [4]
Isaac Watts

KEY POINTS TO REMEMBER.

1. God is jealous for His glory and you can use this as a foundation of your prayers. Think about what gives Him glory.

2. Appeal to his Fathering nature to receive help, don't be independent.

3. Let someone's strength cover your weakness. Andrew was great on the phone that day! That is a strength he has.

4. Supernatural gifts CONFIRM your resolve and faith, expect to see visions. ONCE GOD HAS GIVEN YOU A WORD THE GIFTS JUST ENCOURAGE YOU EVEN MORE.

5. Use your imagination and dare to speak it out. It's almost like painting the future you'd like before it happens.

6. Pray boldly in public and whisper confidently in private. Stay consistent with your confession.

3. GARETH'S MIRACLE

'Some extraordinary thing happens to someone who holds on to the love of God when the odds are totally against Him' [5]
Oswald Chambers

Gareth was a beautiful baby at birth and he quickly grew and gained weight. He showed lots of promise right from the start, however as he entered his fifth week things took a turn for the worse. We had an elderly relative staying with us who became seriously ill with what turned out to be non-infectious meningitis. She was rushed to hospital and against all odds made a remarkable and total recovery within eight weeks.

The baby, however, was given antibiotics because of a cough and as a precaution against meningitis. He quickly began to have skin problems that just would not go away, no matter what cream the doctor prescribed. We don't know if it was the medicine he was given or the stress in the house at the time that made him ill. It could even have been caused by something else completely!

Within a few weeks I found myself at the hospital for three appointments every week, to monitor his condition. By this time he needed steroid creams and bandages from his head to his toes. Nothing seemed to soothe his terribly dry and inflamed skin. I was breastfeeding him, so I took as many precautions with my diet as is possible. I was told this might help to clear the condition.

I had to be careful with our laundry and rinsed the clothes over two dozen times in the machine to get rid of any soap. We never wore wool. All the detergents we had in the house were special non-irritant ones, and the amounts used were cut to a minimum. Pets and animals were banned, and of course there was that old problem of dust! Being a qualified nurse I could bandage and bathe Gareth without much pressure but the situation began to control every area of our lives.

As previously written from Psalms 118 I believe the Bible when it says that, 'It's better to trust in the Lord than to trust in man.' The next verse says 'it's better to trust in the Lord than in princes' (the experts). I believe that medicine is from God and that medical people have been led and inspired by God to help mankind fight disease. However, all this has to bow the knee to Jesus.

I was a trained nurse and I believe in the great work accomplished in hospitals, but I've learned that I need faith to trust people, especially where our health is concerned. Even when going to hospital or the doctor, I focus my faith on God who gives wisdom. I TRUST HIM TO LEAD THE EXPERT TO BRING THE BEST ANSWER FOR US.

I had to listen carefully to what people said to me and then find God's answer in it all. I realised that I needed a green light from God as to what action to take. Was I to go down the hospital route, or travel in a different direction that meant finding the answers from another source? We all have to live with the decisions we make, and so do the people nearest to us. For us God shone a green light to 'go it alone'.

'Your word is a lamp to my feet and a light to my path.' **Psalms 119: 105**

We had less and less confidence in the medical advice given at the time because it was changing from week to week. We thought it through and we decided to withdraw the steroid creams and rely on God for an answer. With so much literature out on the subject and everyone's kind advice the picture became a confusing nightmare. The journey was only just beginning. GARETH NEEDED TWENTY TWO OUT OF TWENTY FOUR HOURS OF TOTAL NURSING CARE, and he managed to sleep for the other two; just about anyway.

I prayed asking God for a remedy that would cure him, not cover up the problem. I WANTED HIM TO BE STRONG, and for his own immune system to recover and carry the workload it was designed to carry. I was concerned for his comfort and I bought many products at the chemist in the hope that they would soothe his hot dry skin. I threw most of the jars away because the lotions and creams were clearly not going to help. Gareth continued to go through a three day cycle where his skin would weep profusely and then it would dry up and flake off in layers. The doctor said it was eczema, and the baby also constantly came up in hives, sometimes all over his body.

His diet was another issue altogether and I asked for advice from the hospital dietician. A strict regime that I'd painstakingly worked out seemed to make him grow at last but I didn't know for sure if there was something missing. It turned out that everything was in there somewhere and Gareth enjoyed it and that was the most important thing.

He had to have his own pans and utensils for food preparation so we took them with us wherever we went! We would know pretty soon if we could relax in a place or not because if

Gareth's skin began to react in any way we'd only be able to stay for five minutes.

Crying through hot tears was the only way I could pray at some points but when God's soothing presence came, I would be encouraged.

'But you, O Lord, are a shield for me, my glory, and the lifter of my head'. **Psalms 3:3**

Friends were a tremendous help at this time, especially with the other three boys. Weeks later we knew an answer would be on its way, because a preacher in another country SPOKE A PROPHETIC WORD OF DIRECTION over Gareth that told of healing. God uses these people and we then have the responsibility of working with the instruction given.

Andrew often brings powerful and specific words like this to people in our Sunday meetings. I kept praying for wisdom and energy as Gareth needed lots of love and specific care so that he could be comfortable, and we waited for the answer.

The book of Samuel records:

'So David went to Baal Perazim, and David defeated them there; and he said, 'The Lord has broken through my enemies before me, like a breakthrough of water.' Therefore he called the name of that place Baal Perazim.' **2 Samuel 5:20 (NKJV)**

The name literally means 'Master of Breakthroughs'. As time went on I became aware that God was highlighting some specific names of herbs that kept appearing in the books I read. God was clearly revealing to me a recipe. I began to think I should dare to make cream for him. Usually I would know within a minute if he could cope with something, because a weal would appear wherever any new substance touched his skin. His skin was so sensitive that he did not tolerate any chemicals or woollen materials at all.

I carefully made the cream to the exact recipe that came to me and tried a tiny spot of it on his foot. There was NO REACTION, which in itself was a miracle. I covered his foot with the cream and we could see it instantly becoming pale, cool and soft whilst the rest of his body was hot, red and itchy. The following day I covered his tiny body in the cream in the morning and then again at night after his baths. For months I'd had to use ordinary cream at least ten times in the morning alone. It would soak into his skin and disappear without any trace or effect at all.

We realised this new cream was working for Gareth and I made more up as needed and froze extra for the winter months. It was so wonderful to have a happy little boy. Once he was happy and comfortable I could begin to look at building up his life, and I also wanted to get to know my little boy who had not really smiled since he was born! He was now ten months old.

For all of those early months he had only grunted in discomfort, he couldn't even cry because all of his energy went into rubbing himself to get rid of the itch. We would often find him bleeding in his cot because he'd been able to somehow get his hands free. He would reach inside his clothes to scratch at his fiery skin for all of those first months of his young life. If you've had a child like this, you know what I'm talking about!

NOW FOR THE FIRST TIME there was the opportunity to develop his diet and social experiences so that he could enjoy life! He had begun his little life with many restrictions but now things were beginning to change for us all, especially for Gareth as his life began to open up wonderfully. We took thoughtful steps week by week and sometimes day by day, and we specifically monitored THE WAY WE TALKED ABOUT THE CHALLENGE.

Taking ground for all the months he had lost was really important. After removing the bandages, once I was confident he wouldn't scratch himself, it looked like his hands would remain clumsy and uncoordinated. I was shocked and felt I'd made some bad choices about his care. He picked everything up with his knuckles and not his finger tips! I asked God for help and within a few days his hands were incredibly strong, normal and very agile.

Praying in the night was the only way ahead at this time and calling on God for every new step became a real habit. Every new thing he ate was checked out in fine detail so I was an expert label-reader in the local shops. All his clothes were cotton, and as you can imagine there were no pets allowed in our house then!

To be comfortable was heaven for him but Gareth's life was still quite contained and lots needed to change for him to grow up happily. We had to put some strategies in place that would help us fight for his freedom from this sensitivity. We literally fought for every new stage of his development. Andrew and I would take it in turns to carry Gareth out into the cool garden air in the middle of the night.

WE AGAIN LEARNED SOME THINGS ABOUT CONFESSION AND OWNERSHIP.

WE SPOKE OF IT AS THOUGH IT WERE A PASSING PHASE and NOT GARETH'S PROBLEM TO OWN OR KEEP FOR LIFE. Lots of people told us that he would never get better in fact they said it would affect him for the rest of his life. They even expected lots more to come his way and we did not like or welcome their well-intended worldly wisdom!

We were particularly aware of the fear factor that had to be resisted at all times and didn't forecast a life of pain or intimidation for our boy. Neither would we let anyone else speak of him like that. It didn't call for argument or rudeness but we were firm in our resistance if anyone tried to impress on us a tale of doom and gloom. People live out of their limited experience and that is not a safe or secure place for you to build your future hopes and desires.

> *'Deliver me and rescue me from the hands of foreigners whose mouths are full of lies whose right hands are deceitful. Then our sons in their youth will be like well-nurtured plants, and our daughters will be like pillars carved to adorn a palace.'*
> **Psalms 144:11-12 (NIV)**

This psalm tells us to ask God to rescue us from the power of words that talk us into defeat and discouragement. Our children's welfare and success depend on it. It is important that you understand the power of agreement here because things are confirmed in the mouth of two witnesses. You are also more likely to stick at it if there is the encouragement of another faith-filled person alongside you, causing the answer to be inevitable. Discord and clamour do not bring resolve, no matter how desperate you are.

'Again I tell you, if two of you on earth agree (harmonize together, make symphony together) about whatever [anything and everything] they may ask, it will be come to pass and be done for them by My Father in heaven. For wherever two or three are gathered (drawn together as My followers) in (into) My name, there I AM in the midst of them.' **Matthew 18:19-20**

If we can stay alongside someone of like-minded faith a force is released that the enemy cannot withstand. Unity and agreement cause a commanded blessing.

'Behold, how good and how pleasant it is for brethren to dwell together in unity! It is like the precious ointment poured on the head, that ran down on the beard, even the beard of Aaron [the first high priest], that came down upon the collar and skirts of his garments [consecrating the whole body]. It is like the dew of [lofty] Mount Hermon and the dew that comes on the hills of Zion; for there the Lord has commanded the blessing, even life forevermore [upon the high and the lowly].' **Psalms 133:1-3**

God's almighty power is released when we agree as we pray together over things that concern us, and His blessing is poured on us like oil in these circumstances. The pressure is eased and the cogs are oiled for things to move swiftly and freely, without friction and aggravation.

With all my heart I wanted Gareth to be well and to live a normal and happy childhood and I found great comfort and strength in words like:

'Delight yourself also in the Lord, and He will give you the desires and secret petitions

of your heart. Commit your way to the Lord [roll and repose each care of your load on Him]; trust (lean on, rely on, and be confident) also in Him and He will bring it to pass.' **Psalms 37:4-5**

I knew that trusting God would severely affect how long it took for the answer to come through. During these months of using the cream, lots of time and effort were needed to introduce Gareth to new foods and materials that previously he couldn't go near. YET MY NEXT CHALLENGE WAS GOING TO CAUSE ME TO REALLY CHECK WHERE MY FAITH HAD BEEN PLACED ALONG THE JOURNEY. HAD I MOVED GOD OVER, FOR A WHILE?

One day at the stove where I was already cooking up more cream, God spoke to me again and told me not to use the cream and that Gareth did not need it any more. It seemed a huge step to take after we'd witnessed the tremendous relief that it had brought. After discussing the situation with Andrew, I knew I really must trust this and obey the new instruction.

I became very aware of how easy it is to settle and rest on an answer that was definitely God-given in the first place. It was difficult to remove this routine from our lives and I realised that once again my trust must be in God and not in the thing that seemed to be working at the time. IT WAS CLEARLY A GOD-GIVEN MIRACLE BUT I NEEDED TO TRUST THE GOD OF THE MIRACLE, NOT PLACE MY TRUST IN THE MIRACLE ITSELF! It's like having a signpost which, although it carries great news and hope of the destination, is still not the destination.

At the time I had quite an inward battle for a few hours, but the new promptings to stop using the cream proved to be the way forward. I never have used it on him again. And he has certainly never needed it since or any other cream at all. He bathes with bubble bath, eats what he likes and loves to play with the cat!

THIS MIRACLE WAS SENT FROM HEAVEN IF EVER THERE WAS ONE!

A few years ago we were given a newspaper which contained the story of a young woman with terrible allergies. Her beginnings and early infanthood mirrored Gareth's story. SHE'D GROWN UP TO NEED AND DEPEND ON SEVENTY INJECTIONS EVERY DAY AND STILL COULDN'T JOIN IN WITH ORDINARY PASTIMES. SHE WAS COMPLETELY HEMMED IN AND COCOONED IN HER TRAUMA. She could not mix with friends or eat any normal food without huge repercussions.

One of the main reasons why we decided to stop using prescribed creams was the fact that we wanted Gareth's own system to be strong. We felt that with God's help we could build up his body's own ability to deal with things that at one time had given him a problem.

The shop-bought and professionally prescribed creams seemed to push his strength into decline and cause him to lose his grip on ever being free of needing them. Even though it was a step of faith to withdraw this treatment we felt assured that because God had clearly said to do it, then He would be with us along the way.

I REALISE NOW THAT ONCE THE DECISION WAS MADE AND WE WERE

TOTALLY RELYING ON GOD IT WAS THEN THAT THE ANSWER CAME!

You have to be pretty determined to follow through with the instruction that God brings your way. God wants so much for you to be victorious and for your enemy to be utterly destroyed. Going to a prayer line for healing can look like a habit to some people, yet I believe you must never stop seeking that complete breakthrough until God tells you to.

You must never give up on God because you may just be a moment away from your miracle. You must never become soft and accepting of the thing that is trying to defeat you, but you must fight until it is utterly finished. In that Old Testament story of David's fight with Goliath, he didn't just knock the big brute down and walk away happy. HE TOOK GOLIATH'S HEAD OFF! NOT A PRETTY SIGHT.

> *'Then David put his hand in his bag and took out a stone; and he slung it and struck the Philistine in his forehead, so that the stone sank into his forehead, and he fell on His face to the earth. So David prevailed over the Philistine with a sling and a stone, and struck the Philistine and killed him. But there was no sword in the hand of David. Therefore David ran and stood over the Philistine, took his sword and drew it out of its sheath and killed him, and cut off his head with it. And when the Philistines saw that their champion was dead, they fled.'*
> **1 Samuel 17:49-51 (NKJV)**

WOW. THAT'S DEALING WITH THE ISSUE AT HAND! Most people would be happy for a little peace and quiet thinking that it's enough to knock the enemy out. But we must destroy the force that tries to crush us. At the same time when other enemies see how severe we are they'll flee as well.

David left nothing to chance, and completely annihilated the force that was trying to mock him and his God! I believe more of us need to view our enemy like this, so that we do not give any room for the thing to rise again. A violent, tenacious force will take the thing and beat it down into defeat.

Getting healed is one thing, keeping our healing is another. The company we keep and the things we inadvertently agree with affect our ongoing success more than we realise. Let's sharpen up and get wise to keep what we've already won.

'Quitting is a permanent solution to a temporary problem.' **Anon**

KEY POINTS TO REMEMBER.

1. Find people to agree with when praying over an issue, people who believe with you and for you.

2. Expect good things for your children and talk positively about them and in front of them.

3. Don't fall for the trick that tells you you're failing if you've to go back to the prayer line again. Push through the pride and embarrassment. The enemy wants you to give up. Don't do it.

4. Walk through each day carefully and ask for God's wisdom when wanting to take new ground.

5. Aim for the best long term answer in the situation. Not a quick fix that's easy to come by. Get God's word on it! We wanted Gareth to be comfortable and for him the steroid cream brought no real relief. We could have been content with how he was, but then missed the freedom he now enjoys. He does not use any medication and has no need of special creams. God is good!

4. CRIME DOESN'T PAY

We live in a world swamped in a materialistic culture and it's easy to find people who are driven to gain wealth and gather exotic possessions. In itself this is not wrong, but if it's all we live for then something will eventually break! Somehow people have fallen for the lie that says you are secure if you have wealth. They place unmerited trust in their 'healthy' bank balance. All too often they come crashing down because real security was never there.

On the other hand some individuals run away from money and the whole subject of prosperity, because to them it carries with it the ugly sound of greed and self gratification. I believe that having plenty is simply an opportunity to give more away. God will, in fact, increase the wealth of a person with this kind of outlook.

Beware of the comfort zone mentality that says 'I'm fine thank you' yet does nothing to help when someone else faces severe hardship. Or the voice that says all is well, while the gospel stays under wraps or is silenced because of lack of support and financial investment. The world is waiting for us to plan and fund His cause with real money. There is a lot of sparkle and dazzling entertainment for people to be seduced by. The TV and the magazines are full of eye-catching material, yet sadly many have offered the priceless jewel of eternal life in a paltry form.

TAKE HEART; THINGS ARE CHANGING, AND RAPIDLY TOO!
I believe that when I grow in wealth, my potential to give is increased and God's

expectation of me to give is multiplied, and I can actually give more. I am released to do something, as well as pray for someone. I AM RELEASED TO PUT MY COMMITMENT MORE FULLY INTO THE PROMOTION OF THE GOSPEL. IT IS THE ONLY MESSAGE THAT OFFERS ETERNAL LIFE!

Yet God does not expect me to despise and misuse the things He prospers me with. I need to be a good steward and that means I have to go and get back what the enemy thought he could steal from me. I have to protect and care for the things I have.

> 'A saint doesn't know the joy of the Lord in spite of tribulation, but because of it.'[6]
> **Oswald Chambers**

Living in a city has the usual challenges of noise and crime. Our house had been broken into and burgled at least three times and now we came home to find the fourth occasion facing us. Andrew and I were disappointed, and we complained to the Lord. We then cleared the broken glass and scanned the place to see what was missing this time.

The CID came along to search for fingerprints and on finding none told us to forget about our stolen goods. They also spoke to our neighbours, who were victims of the same crime spree. WE PRAYED AND ASKED GOD TO DO SOMETHING IN WHAT SEEMED A NO WIN SITUATION.

The following week Andrew was in his city centre office and he felt a strong prompting from God to walk to the other side of the city. After wondering why and how long it would take on this very busy day, he quickly began to work his way to a shopping arcade across the city. He stood outside an antique shop. Andrew thought that he was supposed to meet someone whom God was sending his way for a 'special' appointment, that's happened to him a few times in years gone by. It wasn't part of the agenda for this day, as you'll see. When he stepped inside the shop to find there were no other customers, he pondered why he was there. He looked around and admired the articles in the cabinets and then it happened! One of the watches looked amazingly familiar. IT WAS HIS, AND NEXT TO IT WAS A BROOCH OF MINE!

He was shocked to find himself looking at our belongings neatly lined up on a display shelf. Days before there had been no hope of justice or retrieval but now some of our things were within reach. Right then he needed wisdom to know what to do. We knew where it all came from, but how had it arrived in this place? As he prayed again, Andrew came up with a plan! He asked the shopkeeper to put the watch aside as he needed to go to the bank. He would withdraw cash and then return to buy it.

Instead of going to the bank he went into the nearest police station and began to tell them the story. It took some time for them to be convinced that this was true and although they were unsure they called our local CID. They found the whole story quite incredible, and were reluctant to believe at first, but they told Andrew what to do next!

During the following moments things got very exciting as the police returned to the shop with him. They asked him to pretend to buy our stolen belongings back, so that they could come and interrupt the transaction. Then they could question the shopkeeper about handling stolen goods

They had not believed it when Andrew told them the story of the break-in and how our anger turned into a prayer that God would do something on our behalf to bring the things back. They were amazed at such an unusual story and were very pleased to be involved. What a tale they now had to tell their pals at the pub!

Even more unusual was the fact that they traced more of our things that were being stored elsewhere.

The shopkeeper pleaded his innocence, and to prove it said that he always kept a note of the suppliers' details. At this point the police said this was the end of the trail. But THE THIEF HAD GIVEN HIS REAL NAME AND ADDRESS to this shop owner. He was immediately traced, together with more of our belongings, and things that had been stolen from our neighbours and another thirty crime scenes.

WE LEARNED THAT DAY THAT EVEN STOLEN PROPERTY IS IMPORTANT TO THE LORD, AND THAT OUR GOD SEES AND IS CONCERNED WITH THAT WHICH CONCERNS US. IT WAS GREAT TO BE IN A POSITION THAT BROUGHT A POSITIVE OUTCOME TO A NEGATIVE SITUATION.

This was not the end of the saga either. It all happened at a time when the BBC wanted to produce a documentary for television about answered prayer. They stated that stories of people being healed were old hat and that they wanted to use something more exciting!

Our story was so unusual that it was re-enacted for the cameras, and we were able to tell it to millions of viewers. We love it when God gets the glory. It was clearly His intervention that turned it all around.

THAT'S not even the end of the story!

A few months later our son was in his class at school when his teacher called a debate on the power and authenticity of the supernatural. First though, they would watch a video of a BBC documentary on which they would base their discussion!

You guessed it! They used that same BBC documentary as the focal point for the whole lesson. As pupils laughed at the incredulous stories, our son was able to state confidently that it was true and that our family was featured. Amazingly the teacher's own family were also involved on the video as part of another item that showed divine intervention.

WHAT A HAT TRICK!

God is interested. He is willing and able to help us. He will surely get His Glory!

'The Lord is on my side; I will not fear. What can man do to me?' **Psalm 118:6**

KEY POINTS TO REMEMBER!

1. God hears you when you pray.

2. He does not want you to lose things and simply let go of them.

3. Be real, tell the Lord if you're disappointed and ask Him for His help.

4. He is hungry for glory and acclaim and will use your life to get it. Even the things that seem negative to you can bring Him fame, if you will yield them to Him.

5. God will do far more than you can imagine if you will give Him the room to move in His way. So often we try to tell God how to answer our prayers when He just wants us to give the situation over to Him.

5. SIMEON'S STORY

'It is the Holy Spirit who gives us revelation and conviction as to the true nature of the attack'[7]
Arthur Wallis

Simeon is known for his amazing energy and people often comment on his wonderful zest for life. He never stops moving and greets most of life with more than the usual dose of enthusiasm.

On waking one morning eleven weeks after giving birth to him, I distinctly heard a prompting to check his temperature. No time was set on it and I didn't feel the urgency to do it there and then, but I watched him carefully all day. He fed well as usual and slept peacefully. He seemed healthy and content. He was a beautiful baby and I loved to hug and hold him near. As the day unfolded however I realised something was not right. HIS COLOUR CHANGED AND HE SEEMED TO BE DIFFERENT. Even so Simeon did not have a high temperature.

The previous weekend we'd been away with our friend who is a paediatrician. During one of our many conversations she'd commented that it's not easy to tell if or why a newborn baby is unwell, other than by touch. Holding the baby would give indication of tension and changes in health. The tests done on adults don't always reveal problems when carried out on new babies.

I became concerned and decided to call her for some advice. I was relieved to find her at another friend's home. She just happened to be spending some time-off there, and was not far away. On cradling him, she said that SIMEON

WAS UNWELL. She advised me to take him to the doctor.

I TOOK HIM TO THE GP who thought that the problem was an ear infection. I was not sure and I had begun to think his tummy was tender. When I mentioned it to the Doctor she examined his abdomen. He let out a scream and I was told to take him to the hospital as soon as possible.

On arrival at the hospital the surgeons met us at the door. Simeon was collapsing and they needed to put IV lines in, which was very difficult on such a tiny baby. They expected to operate on his bowel because they thought it was twisted. They thought that it needed to be surgically unravelled!

I kept saying that he'd fed well, and had filled his nappy as normal. I had noticed, though, that he hadn't wet his nappy very much that day. I felt they were going down the wrong diagnostic route. Something didn't seem to make sense, and after countless tests that night they found that he had a urine infection.

Thank God he was spared the surgery. The hospital staff had been quite bemused as I had held on to Simeon and told him that 'HE WAS MINE AND GOING NOWHERE'. During the evening he collapsed more than once. Andrew had been unaware of the trauma that we were facing and arrived at hospital late on the evening. We had some time to talk, pray for Simeon and then he had to leave to take care of the other four boys at home. My friend had been faithfully holding the fort whilst we were not there.

Not wanting to leave him for a moment I sat with Simeon for hours praying and believing God for a total breakthrough. Later in the middle of the night I needed to change position, visit the bathroom and move around for a little while! I returned from a brief tea break to find that Simeon was settled and asleep at last. YET I KNEW I MUST HOLD HIM. Right then I knew I had to be in close contact with him for comfort and to pray for him. I felt quite urgent about it.

To the nurse's dismay, we inevitably woke him up as I insisted she lifted him from her lap onto mine. Within moments I was reminded of the prompting that had come twenty-four hours earlier to check his temperature, and I immediately called the nurse to see how he was doing. He did feel very hot.

Instantly we saw that the reading was 42'C and we knew this was potentially disastrous for him. Once again, the hospital staff had to race around to bring the help he needed and within a short while this new crisis was over. Over the next two days it became evident that Simeon was also suffering from septicaemia (blood poisoning), which is a terrible and potentially fatal disease for the strongest of individuals, never mind a new baby.

We praise God for His whispered instruction and the grace to follow it through at the right time. My doctor friend later told me that if I'd gone to the GP sooner the baby's sickness could have been misdiagnosed and then mistreated. Also, because I probably would have put my trust in the medicine given, I wouldn't have felt at liberty to go back again, and Simeon could have died in the night.

I DO BELIEVE GOD SPEAKS CLEARLY and on hearing His voice WE WILL ALSO BE

GIVEN THE WISDOM TO WORK WITH THE INSTRUCTION, AT THE RIGHT TIME.

Sometimes we run in life, as if when in a crisis, and sometimes we walk in life as if when we're weary. Our father God wants us to soar through it all. He will cause us to rise up above the immediate circumstance to see it through His eyes. We'll also be nearer to Him and therefore more able to hear that still small voice.

I ALSO REALISED THAT I HAD TO BE CAREFUL WITH THE WORDS I SPOKE. We must know that whatever is happening in our world, our words are powerful. We need to know that we can have what we say and therefore we must only say what we truly want, and nothing else. Our words carry creative power and even what you and I say can produce dramatic effects in our lives. I constantly told Simeon, 'You are mine and you're not leaving me', even though things looked terrible at times. On the way to the hospital I'd thought he was dying. Yet I couldn't speak it out, it was potentially disastrous.

We also face times when we must wait in silence, if we're not sure of what to say or do.

> *'FOR GOD alone my soul waits in silence; from Him comes my salvation. He only is my Rock and my Salvation, my Defense and my Fortress, I shall not be greatly moved.'*
> **Psalms 62:1-2**

> *'My soul, wait only upon God and silently submit to Him; for my hope and expectation are from Him.'* **Psalms 62:5**

It's better to say nothing than speak the wrong thing! We must not be afraid to wait. All the while, the Lord is setting things up to bless us, and we must trust him even in the seemingly dark and silent times of our journey.

If we speak in tongues (this is another gift of God that empowers us today), we must do this often as it builds us up and does something in our spirit to prepare us for the fight. It sharpens us and causes us to be more effective with our strategy and decision-making skills.

I ALSO BEGAN TO REALISE THAT I HAD TO STAY ALERT.

I could have breathed a sigh of relief when the baby was asleep at last, but even in the middle of the night I was reminded to check his temperature right there and then. I had to wake him up, WHICH WAS AGAINST MY NATURAL INSTINCT AS A MOTHER.

I wanted to sleep, Simeon was peaceful and needed to sleep and the nurse was also pleased that he was settled. I had to cut through it all to follow through with the conviction that I must check his temperature. I knew I must!

I THANK GOD OFTEN BECAUSE HE DOES GIVE WISDOM TO US ALL, WHEN WE ASK.

'I will bless the Lord, who has given me counsel; yes my heart instructs me in the night seasons. I have set the Lord continually before me; because He is at my right hand, I shall not be moved. Therefore my heart is glad and my glory [my inner self] rejoices; my body too shall rest and confidently dwell in safety.' **Psalms 16:7-9**

'And the LORD will make you the head and not the tail; you shall be above only, and not be beneath, if you heed the

commandments of the LORD your God, which I command you today, and are careful to observe them.'
Deuteronomy 28: 13 (NKJV)

This tells me that I'm supposed to be at the deciding and initiating end of the game. The part that sees, hears and talks! Not the part that tags on at the end of the picture, and which always follows the lead given by someone else.

The doctors were about to operate on our son and it would have put far too much pressure on his body. It wasn't the right answer for this situation. I prayed passionately for the medical team involved that God would help them with their investigations and for them to make good choices.

I THANK the Lord for them and their gifts and skills, which are God given. Some are great and some are small and I especially TRUST the God who gave them.

When we're involved with the kingdom of God we do have enemies who try to throw a spanner in the works. We must keep our wits about us at all times and not give an inch. Simeon was saved and we were able to take him home a few days later. Today he has more energy and passion for life than anyone I know and he's just seven years old!

'Never accept the negative until you have thoroughly explored the positive.' **Anon**

KEY POINTS TO REMEMBER.

1. When you sense a conviction give it space to grow. Don't just dismiss it, but pray it through and talk it over with God.

2. Get confident in hearing God speak to you. Have a believing heart and dare to trust that it's His voice.

3. Even when experts say that they know better, if you are sure that God has given you other information tell them about it graciously! Sometimes they will not understand but when you're dealing with people's lives you must be strong. It's always a sobering thought that we live with the decisions we make and the expert isn't always there to help us through later on. However God is always there for us.

4. Begin by practicing with the small things in life, God is good and He'll not rush you into major decisions right from the beginning.

5. When wisdom comes ask God about when and how to use it, so you can secure the best outcome.

6. BORN FOR THIS

'It is essential that we seek God's face and train ourselves to listen.'[8] **Arthur Wallis**

Years ago we took a break with relatives in the beautiful north of Scotland. Having rested and spent time together as a family you would imagine that all was well and that nothing was amiss in our lives. Yet all was not well with my soul as I meandered through another season of wondering if I had a part to play, and if I was equipped to do the tasks at hand. The challenge to be a superwoman in marriage, motherhood and leadership was pressing heavily on me at the time. I was trying to find identity and value and a place of belonging. These are needs that many people have at some stage of their journey.

Life for each of us has its own unique battles and joys, and I was contemplating some of this during our short holiday away from home. I woke early to the sound of the postman bringing the mail to the post office next door. I hadn't slept much that night really and I felt that I'd been carrying the world on my shoulders.

To get up was a blessing and I was determined to bring all of these concerns to the Lord. I knew that I couldn't keep going round in rings with these thoughts and that something must be settled, once and for all. The enemy does not want us to succeed but as we remember that God is for us and he is willing us to win we can move forward again with strength, and boldness. To allow the troublesome thoughts of doubt to deter us can affect our advancement and influence.

If we do not deal with negativity it will deal with us. It takes away our confidence in the goodness of God. It causes us to feel abandoned even when we know that He has promised to never leave us or let us down. The Bible states this clearly:

> *'No man shall be able to stand before you all the days of your life. As I was with Moses, so I will be with you; I will not fail you or forsake you.'* **Joshua 1:5**

There are voices within and enemies from without that we must recognise and deal with. The story of Nehemiah in the Bible tells us very clearly about how important it is to continue with the job even during tremendous conflict. I think I'll write on that score next time! People sometimes come close to us when we're in difficulties and they seem to be a help to us. Yet really what they are trying to do is hold us back in those problem zones while they look for ways in which to shine. Someone once said that it's like a person who lights their own candle to make it to shine brighter while the other person's candle is blown out in the process. Women face many challenges as they seek to be the best that they can be.

There are so many role models in life, especially those seen on TV, and those we read of in magazines and newspapers. Having relatives or colleagues that seem to ooze confidence and show tremendous ability also can be such a challenge to live up to. When you're a woman in leadership and you're aiming to become all that God has planned for you, then you have to deal with the challenges and pressures to become superwoman. Not all women have risen to the opportunity and privilege and some are still working on it. We must remember that God said He'd never leave us if we follow on in His word for direction.

Life is a journey and not everyone wants to take this route or chooses to walk with us for the whole of the distance. It's disappointing when we don't reach the finish line together, and many are just a moment away from receiving the prize. GOD WANTS US ALL TO CROSS THE FINISHING LINE. However, where we are, and with who, can make all the difference to the pace that we set and our final destination and rewards.

We need one another in many types of relationships. Some will be close friends, and some will be associates. Many will be acquaintances that we meet for just a short while yet I do believe God is bringing us together in unique partnerships that will carry significance in the days ahead. We need to differentiate between all of these to make wise choices as to who fits where.

On this frosty February morning I realised that I'd fallen foul of the words spoken by others as they'd seen me go through some tough times. I now needed to pray concerning their testimony over my life.

'But they who wait for the Lord shall renew their strength, they shall mount up with wings like eagles, they shall run and not be weary, they shall walk and not faint.'
Isaiah 40:31 (RSV)

It also says that even when youths faint and get weary, we will be the ones who are strong. It is from God that we draw our best strength. We need to know how to strengthen ourselves and at the right time draw in encouragement from others too. In the Bible we find that King David of the Old Testament took time to encourage himself:

> 'And David was greatly distressed; for the people spoke of stoning him, because all the people were bitter in soul, each for his sons and daughters. But David strengthened himself in the Lord his God.'
> **1 Samuel 30:6 (RSV)**

Earlier we see that David also needed his friend whose words brought life to his sagging heart.

> 'And David was afraid because Saul had come out to seek his life. David was in the Wilderness of Ziph at Horesh. And Jonathan, Saul's son rose, and went to David at Horesh, and strengthened his hand in God.' **1 Samuel 23:15-16 (RSV)**

THIS ENCOURAGEMENT CAN BE GREAT BUT YOU MUST WATCH OUT BECAUSE CARING PEOPLE CAN SOMETIMES LOVE YOU TO DEATH! There's a difference between being strengthened and your need being commiserated with. Every time they say how tired you look or question you on your position in the fight they have highlighted your need. (It would be better that they pray for you and just lift some undue weight from your shoulders.)

If all your friends do is talk about the situation as though it were too big as you negotiate life, they're giving the enemy a target and you've just become it. A DROWNING MAN DOESN'T NEED TO DISCUSS HOW DEEP, COLD OR WET THE WATER IS. HE JUST NEEDS SOMEONE TO HAUL HIM OUT ONTO DRY LAND! If the pastoral or counselling situation in your life keeps pulling you back to the waters edge, move to a safer place with someone who's escaped onto dry ground before you.

People in leadership have to see this for what it is. The Devil knows that to disrupt or undermine a person will cause havoc. To get involved with a leader and undermine his or her strength under the guise of caring and understanding will affect the whole church. If you want to help you can, by building in faith, by focussing on the truth and by serving in practical ways.

Words are powerful and creative in your life and what someone says of you (not even to your face or in your hearing) can affect your destiny if you allow it. On that cold wintry day in February 1994 I PRAYED IN ORDER TO CUT OFF THE INFLUENCE OF THOSE NEGATIVE WORDS. I DECIDED INSTEAD TO BUILD ON MORE POSITIVE TRUTHS AND PROMISES THAT WOULD BRING AND PRESERVE LIFE.

I began to recall what God had said about my life. There have been prophesies concerning travel and influence and of singing the song of the Lord. I had lived carefully with this sense of calling always at the back of my mind.

Even when one of the toddlers was having a temper tantrum in the supermarket, I would endeavour to handle the situation in a decent and quiet manner. Always trying not to draw attention to the escapade because some day people may get to know us and remember the incident. We are not expected to be perfect but it's good to value the path you know you're about to take and honour God as best as you can from the beginning.

I often used to say to friends that they should practice ruling their children in the home first. It's not good to find out that your small child doesn't hear and obey you in a public, or worse still a dangerous place. For their safety, these things need to be settled when each child is young, and they take time to establish. Bad behaviour can not be ignored and it must be addressed as each child grows through the different stages! I do not believe though that a leader's or pastor's child should be made into an example for everyone else to examine. That would be highly unfair on all the kids in the gang!

On that day, I began to realise that my insecurities were not from God and that it was time to sort things out. I needed a good clear-out of all the junk that had cluttered up my thinking. I began to say sorry for allowing this trash to dog my life and to thank God for this wonderful opportunity to serve Him. It really has been a total adventure.

I remembered a prophecy that was given on our wedding day that spoke of the strength that God would put into us both as individuals. We were encouraged to pool these strengths and partner together. There were words that told us that we would stand in situations which would have caused many others to fall.

I realised that I was God's perfect choice for my husband because others could never have stood the tests that we'd been through and still come out ready to fight and take more ground. Many would have become distracted or disheartened and given up, BUT WHEN YOU'RE BORN TO BE PIONEERS THE OPTION TO QUIT IS NOT ON THE MENU OR PART OF THE AGENDA.

The enemy had been relentless in trying to affect my confidence and my sense of positioning and ownership of the role God had called me into. Everyone else was oblivious to these repetitive thoughts that I had.

That morning, we all had breakfast and said our goodbyes. We were in for a shock as we journeyed home to Glasgow. IT WAS VERY ICY AND THE ROADS WERE COVERED IN FROST, the air was crisp but at times it was thick with freezing fog. We were almost an hour into our journey when we saw a hold-up ahead and had to break hard to stop and avoid the truck in front of us.

The lorry behind was travelling far too fast and could not slow down in time. He was hurtling toward us and I can imagine the driver's horror as he began to realise there were two boys in the rear-facing seat of our car.

JUST BEFORE IMPACT, THE CAR RANG WITH THE SOUND OF US CALLING OUT FOR PROTECTION. I KNEW WE WOULD BE SAFE because of the sense of hope and promise that had been instilled into me that morning very early on. Remember, I'd been talking to God before dawn!

In the confusion there was a lot of noise and jostling around for a few moments before everything went silent. Our little boys wondered what was happening when they saw that we were now sandwiched between two huge juggernauts.

Just then a mist covered the car as two more vehicles smashed into the side of us. One of them went right over our roof. We couldn't get out at first and had to smash the windows to climb through. The roof was buckled and we could smell petrol!

After we'd managed to scramble out we still had to reach for the children and lift them free. Each one of them (we had four then) was checked for injury and found to be perfectly fine. Apart from seatbelt burns and slight bruising, NO ONE WAS INJURED! The side where the car took the brunt of the impact just happened to be where we'd put the seat down to store the buggy. IT WAS BENT AND TOTALLY USELESS.

The boys in the back concerned me, because I wondered how they'd cope with the memory of seeing the juggernaut racing toward them. I didn't want them to have nightmares. It was totally amazing because we actually had to wake them up so that they could be helped to climb out. THEY HAD SLEPT PEACEFULLY through the whole incredible incident and were completely unaware of the smash we'd just been in. THE CAR WAS TOTALLY WRITTEN OFF BUT NOT ONE OF US NEEDED AN X-RAY AND WE WERE SENT HOME ON THE TRAIN, AS THOUGH THIS WAS PART OF THE HOLIDAY!

The emergency teams said that we were the 'luckiest' people they'd seen through what had been a day of multiple crashes on that stretch of road! Little did they know just Who it was that stepped in to save us all!

'Because you have made the Lord your refuge, and the Most High your dwelling place, There shall no evil befall you, nor any plague or calamity come near your tent. For He will give His angels [especial] charge over you to accompany and defend and preserve you in all your ways [of

obedience and service]. They shall bear you up on their hands, lest you dash your foot against a stone.' **Psalms 91: 9-12**

I remember praying for those in the cars and trucks all around us and to my knowledge no one was very seriously hurt in the crash that we were involved in. After that the emergency and police officials closed the road until the weather improved. I know that God arrested my attention that day to remind me of His purpose for my life and His choosing of me for the task.

LIFE IS NOT A GAME and we must be faithful and responsible with the call of God on our lives. We were saved to continue to serve Him. I know that everything we have faced is for a purpose and only we can do the job that we are called to do. WE'RE ALIVE TODAY TO GIVE HIM GLORY.

If we're fearful or unwilling then we leave a gap in the net that God is weaving. It's the same for you and for your life! When it comes to marriage God never sets the scene to move you on so that someone else can come in to take your place. He asks you to work it out and walk in it. Only the enemy deceives and destroys. GOD GIVES KEYS FOR PARTNERSHIP AND RECONCILIATION.

People have often said that they stayed together for the sake of the children. God has a better plan and that plan is about building a strong marriage. A marriage with two awesome people who are PARTNERING TOGETHER IN HIS PURPOSES AND WHO CARRY HIS DESIGNER LABEL ON THEM.

'But you are a chosen race, a royal priesthood, a dedicated nation, [God's] own purchased, special people, that you

may set forth the wonderful deeds and display the virtues and perfections of Him Who called you out of darkness into His marvellous light.'   **1 Peter 2: 9**

Working with people of like heart and partnering with God together will truly lead to ultimate success. Praying over it wisely and being willing to be taught some keys and good principles will make such a great difference. We should spend time with people who have taken the same route, thought the same thoughts and said the same words. People who at one time made the same mistakes, yet now they're different, set free and reaping all the benefits.

Families are not transformed because they attend meetings together and appear on the scene as perfect units each week. The preached word brings knowledge and that is great. BUT THERE IS MORE!

IN THIS PURSUIT OF SUCCESSFUL PEOPLE AND BLOSSOMING FAMILIES, WHEN THE WORD OF GOD IS PREACHED, THE KNOWLEDGE IS SET ON FIRE BY THE VERY PRESENCE OF GOD. AFTER THIS DIVINE EXPERIENCE NOTHING STAYS THE SAME, BECAUSE THIS KNOWLEDGE BECOMES REVELATION.

It's as if they stood tall and hitched up into a crowd that could SHOW THEM this better way. Revelation is revealed truth that changes perspective; THE LIGHT LITERALLY COMES ON!

When there is a desperate need for change, it could be that you need to step into a crowd whose pace and direction is set toward heaven. Then it's easier to move freely and walk forward together with them. Some of these very steps are the processes that will bring salvation to your life. They are the only way to change the scenery of your past memories and hoped for future experiences.

Our society spends billions on rescuing animals and the environment, how about us valuing one another's families? The church is God's rescue operation for mankind. We are to be salt and light. We are the folks to put the zing and brightness back into society in a healthy and righteous way. Very few families avoid difficulty at some point, statistics tell us that. And we all know people who have suffered because of low self esteem or split relationships. Yet we don't need to become one of those statistics nor do we have to stay there in that predicament. You have to arrest your thinking; that is, stop yourself in your tracks and change your own thought processes.

'For the weapons of our warfare are not physical [weapons of flesh and blood], but they are mighty before God for the overthrow and destruction of strongholds. [Inasmuch as we] refute arguments and theories and reasonings and every proud and lofty thing that sets itself up against the [true] knowledge of God; and we lead every thought and purpose away captive into the obedience of Christ (the Messiah, the anointed one), Being in readiness to punish every [insubordinate for his] disobedience, when your own submission and obedience [as a church] are fully secured and complete.' **2 Corinthians 10:4-6**

This tells us about warfare that does not involve bombs and guns, yet it can be just as overpowering when it comes to destroying our enemies. We pulverise enemies which are disguised as broken relationships or that are hidden beneath devastated pasts. It takes a lot of obedience and tenacity to retrain your thinking but it is possible. It brings immense breakthrough and victory into lives that could have been rendered powerless. God declares over every one of His offspring that we were born to carry influence. WE CAN CHOOSE TO TAKE ANOTHER ROUTE and believe that it truly does lead to life.

GETTING INTO PRAYER WITH GOD CAN TURN YOUR DAY, EVEN YOUR LIFE AROUND AS YOU LET HIM SHOW YOU HIS PERSPECTIVE ON IT.

Even if praying is new to you please be assured that God hears you. He wants you to rise above the mundane and aim for excellence, He wants you to rise higher than you could have ever imagined.

> *'Seek the Lord while He may be found, call upon Him while He is near; let the wicked forsake his way, and the unrighteous man his thoughts; let him return to the Lord, that He may have mercy on him, and to our God, for he will abundantly pardon.'*
> **Isaiah 55: 6-8 RSV**

> *'You know my downsitting and my uprising; You understand my thought afar off. You sift and search out my path and my lying down, and you are acquainted with all my ways. For there is not a word in my tongue [still unuttered], but, behold, O Lord, You know it altogether.'* **Psalms 139:2-4**

There's nothing you could ever have done that has written you off forever. There's nothing you could do to shock Him and He longs to help you to find your purpose for living.

'God does not expect perfection; He expects obedience. And through obedience He can turn failures into triumphs....Develop your own style. No one has had the life experiences you have had: no one has the contributions to make that you can make. So it's not a question of being better than someone else. Excellence demands that you be better than yourself.'[9] **Ted W Engstrom**

KEYS TO REMEMBER.

1. God wants you to know that no-one can replace your position in the family. He put you there for a purpose.

2. Allow Him to talk to you about things like this. Learn to encourage yourself, and sometimes seek encouragement from others.

3. Settle things in your heart once and for all, so that when trouble comes to try to shake or destroy you, you have more than enough within you to push it away.

4. In your moment of protection others are protected too when they're near.

5. Realise that the more you've gone through just shows how much God wants you to come through. He's preserved you for a purpose that's bigger than yourself!

6. Don't let other people's love for you slow you down or detract from the focus you should have on your future.

7. HOUSE MOVE (2)

'People who set goals - challenging goals, but goals that are also achievable - are the ones with solid grips on their futures, the ones who end up accomplishing extraordinary things.' [10]

Howard Marguleas

Did you know? It's possible for God to give us the sway over estate agents, and the power that they wield over ordinary people. HE CAN TURN US INTO EXTRAORDINARY PEOPLE. We hit a time when our growing family needed more space so we decided to move house. There are seven of us now, we have been blessed with five sons and we often have lots of visitors coming to stay! We're quite a household and it was time to search for a bigger place.

We looked at details for some lovely places only to find them beyond our reach financially. I began to talk to God about it and I reminded Him that it had been His decision to promise to bring the wealth of the nations to His people. It wasn't just a good idea that some of us had dreamed up, it's actually in the Bible.

'I will shake all the nations, and they will come with the wealth of all nations, and I will fill this house with glory ...'

Haggai 2:7(NASB)

ONE DAY AS I WAS PRAYING IN THE CAR I EXPLODED! As I was driving along the road I noticed a lavishly dressed person coming by with a huge glossy dog on a lead. They were out on a leisurely stroll and looked like the picture of wealth! I was immensely provoked by this display. I POINTED AT THE UNSUSPECTING PERSON (who didn't see me fortunately) and in the middle of my prayer I shouted in the car, 'LORD! YOU'VE PROMISED US MORE AND THAT'S EXACTLY WHAT I'M TALKING ABOUT!'

It was His idea to promise to bless us and we often forget to remind Him. It's always good to keep repeating to God just what He's said He will do for us. Wealth isn't everything and it is not always measured by the things we have. Serving people and loving God are much more important. Having wealth though, can make things happen more easily and quickly.

I carried on driving until I reached home then I began to do the usual housework. When you're a busy woman going for all that God has got for you to do there's no time to stop being practical!

We put things together to get ready to sell the house and I did my best to keep it ready. Life was full and hectic and pretty soon there were a string of estate agents at our door. They came to value our house and we arranged to sell through a particular company, thinking we'd chosen well! We were so pleased when a crowd of viewers came along and a number were keen to take things further. There were a few houses like ours for sale, also with the same agents.

We waited eagerly for news from the agent's office but as time went on it became more a case of them asking me if I had anything to tell them, rather than them giving me any relevant feedback. I was becoming suspicious and impatient, and so I began to pray! Everything seemed to be taking too long and I asked the Lord to show me what was slowing things down. Other properties were selling, and we were not aware of any problem with our place. A few days later I felt God was prompting me to phone the agents to ask them if they had any news. I PHONED IMMEDIATELY!

It was a hot sunny day and when I got through to her office I realised the lady was very relaxed and eating her lunch. She told me of THE OFFER that someone had made and how they (the agents) knew we wouldn't have been interested, so had refused it on our behalf. She also told me the buyer had now actually bought another property, so it was too late!

I asked her if any messages had been left to inform us of this situation and she said, 'no'. I said that Andrew and I would need to talk and we'd be back in touch with her boss! We gave them a little more time to sell (we were far too soft)! Stating that we were not pleased we said we would begin to advertise on our own behalf, and would definitely not pay full fees, due to their bad handling of the sale. OUR OWN PRIVATE ADVERT WENT TO PRINT AS PLANNED.

Two weeks later some folks arrived to take a look at our house having seen our advert in the newspaper. I'd just been trying to help a young neighbour who'd been bitten by a dog that morning and I had a lot on my mind. I really felt that it was important for me not to mention anything about the young person's accident even though I didn't know why.

> *'If any of you is deficient in wisdom, let him ask of the giving God [Who gives] to everyone liberally and ungrudgingly, without reproaching or faultfinding, and it will be given him.'* **James 1:5**

I asked God for His help and then I carried on with the work in the house, unaware of the shock that was coming my way. As I showed them around the house the people told me that they had sold their property only days before, using the same agents that had been working for us. It had been a real struggle for them and they didn't want to deal with those agents again. They were desperate to buy through someone else.

Knowing that they wanted a property within the local vicinity the estate agents had mentioned our place to them on several occasions. However they had not been to view our house because they'd also been dissatisfied with the service given and had decided not to get involved. BUT WHEN THEY SAW OUR OWN PERSONAL ADVERT THEY CHANGED THEIR MINDS!

They came along because we were advertising independently. They actually really liked the area. It turned out that an apparently keen viewer of ours from a few weeks previous had bought their home instead. I was intrigued! I soon became aware that I recognised one of the people and wondered why. I was puzzled at first and then I slowly began to remember.

I could hardly contain my excitement because I began to realise that it was the very same person who had unknowingly provoked my prayers only months before. IT WAS THIS SAME PERSON who I had seen walking down the street with her beautiful clothes and handsome animal. IT WAS THIS PERSON who I had pointed at as I was praying on my journey.

THEY FELL IN LOVE WITH OUR HOUSE, BOUGHT IT AND MOVED IN WITHIN A VERY FEW SHORT WEEKS.

I've wondered if I'd mentioned the little neighbours dog bite if that would have put the buyer's off at all? I don't know! Now I pray over other issues with more determination and I think carefully about what I would really like for our lives. Wisdom, influence and having God's heart seem to me to be the treasures to search for and own.

Many years ago God spoke to me about the fact that WE ALL WANT OUR PRAYERS TO BE ANSWERED. People want and constantly pray for things like a new job or a partner to marry. Sometimes it is for a healing or the salvation of loved ones. He is pleased when we look to Him to provide. He never gets tired of our impatience and faithfully listens to every word and counts the tears. He wants and expects us to come to Him.

Yet the Lord also shared with me His great yearning for mankind. He asked me HOW LONG, DOES HE HAVE TO WAIT TO SEE HIS DREAM FULFILLED. This was God speaking! PEOPLE, HE IS WAITING FOR YOU AND ME. We need to keep things in perspective. Whatever we ask for must never take over from His purposes in our lives. I believe His heart's desire is totally toward the world and its safety and blessing. It is wonderful to think that God has you and me in mind as part of that too.

Back to the humble house!

'So I say to you, ask, and it will be given to you; seek, and you will find; knock, and it will be opened to you. For everyone who asks receives, and he who seeks finds, and to him who knocks, it will be opened.' **Luke 11: 9-10 (NJKV)**

It was amazing how God proved beyond a shadow of a doubt that He hears me when I call on Him. These people bought the house and were moving in within a very few weeks of that first prayer.

In the book of Matthew WE ARE ENCOURAGED TO SEEK FIRST THE KINGDOM OF GOD:

'Therefore do not worry and be anxious, saying, what are we going to have to eat? Or, what are we going to have to drink? Or, what are we going to have to wear? For, the Gentiles (heathen) wish for and crave and diligently seek all these things, and your heavenly Father knows well that you need them all. But, seek (aim at and strive after) first of all, His kingdom and His righteousness (His way of doing and being right), and then all these things taken together will be given you besides.'

Matthew 6:31-33

'Never look back unless you want to go that way.' **Anon**

KEY POINTS TO REMEMBER!

1. The more specific you can be the more God can fine tune the answer.

2. Don't just expect the ordinary for your life. Think out of the box and see how great God is.

3. If you are unsettled about the way things are going, it may be that the Holy Spirit wants you to pray so that you can progress to the next level. Follow the prompting!

4. God can turn an ordinary person into an extraordinary one.

5. Don't forget to carry on with the routine stuff while you're pursuing your breakthrough.

6. If God tells you to be quiet, then be quiet!

8. SCHOOL PLACES

I believe that we all face times when we have to move ahead or take steps into unknown territory. You have to be brave and adventurous whether you're a Christian or not. Whether you believe in fate or the power of prayer can also determine how you view the experience. This also has a great bearing on the outcome. It affects what happens and how easily everyone takes to the transition.

On one occasion we made a move like this and it seemed to be such a challenge to me. I would need new schools for the boys, a new family doctor; in fact everything had to be re-established in our lives. Having seven of us to relocate seemed a daunting task and there were other challenges that I knew we would face in due course.

We were moving into Arden House, the one used for all of the final series of 'DR FINDLAY'S CASEBOOK', a well known TV series. The name is still on the gatepost. Outside there is a lintel that has the date 1711 on it. At the time we were due to move in, it was no longer a sight to behold but quite a job for the builders, plumbers, electricians and all their colleagues.

We knew we couldn't live in it and were in the process of looking at alternative accommodation to see us through the winter. We found a large static caravan for ourselves and the three younger boys, and kind friends gave us a small touring van for the two older boys to sleep in. The washer was to be plumbed into the porch and the drier would be set up in the far corner of the house. I remember trekking backwards and forwards to get washing done, having to carry it in black bin-liners from the house to the caravan. The ironing was kept in check by great girlfriends who used to come along and get stuck in. Sometimes in order to be really spiritual and dynamic in the life of a friend, all we have to do is pick up their ironing!

We had terrible storms that winter and I remember waking in the night on more than one occasion and spending hours praying that we'd not be blown into the local fields. I KNOW WILLIAM WALLACE HAD PLAYED THERE AS A CHILD, and we had bought the house from his descendants but I didn't fancy being introduced to the countryside in this way.

There were lots of things that needed dealing with and as I began to pray I realised that we could not just wait forever. We needed school places within our locality for the children, and I did not want to have to send them in four different directions. However at the time I was told by the educational authorities that the local schools were full and we could have months if not years to wait.

I was encouraged to resign myself and the children to the fact that places were being offered only in other towns! Even on calling to the head office just as the schools were opening after the holidays, the news was the same. I quietly but purposefully told the man in charge that I would be praying, and asked his permission to call again for an update. I KNEW BY THIS STAGE THAT WHEN WE BELONG TO GOD WE CAN MOVE MOUNTAINS!

'For truly I say to you, if you have faith (that is living) like a grain of mustard seed, you can say to this mountain, Move from

here to yonder place, and it will move; and
nothing will be impossible to you.'
Matthew 17:20

By this time we were also fasting often, as we prayed! I had to settle the oldest first because he was to start his third year at secondary school and all eight of his chosen subjects had to be applied for and granted. The school summer holidays were over and I was told that this situation was impossible, as it was just too complicated. Yet once again I took my lead from the word of God and found it in the Bible.

'But thus says the Lord: Even the captives
of the mighty shall be taken away, and the
prey of the terrible be delivered; For I will
contend with him who contends with you,
And I will save your children.'
Isaiah 49:25 (NKJV)

Anything that stops the blessing of God coming towards my family also needs dealing with. As we serve God they inevitably become builders with us and they are in line for breakthroughs and testimonies of their own. THEIR EDUCATION MATTERED TO ME AND THEREFORE TO GOD AS WELL. As I began to pray I knew in my heart that God doesn't do only half a job or provide only the bare minimum. He can more than match any challenge that life brings our way. In fact He's ready for it and more importantly, if we're in His will for our lives, He can't wait to beat all the odds, and show His love and power.

After months of praying I was not going to give in now. I telephoned the school, now that the staff were preparing for the classes to start the following week. I was asked to call again in two days time with the list of subjects that Joshua had chosen. When I read them to the head of department for the third year he laughed with relief and glee as he informed me that the subjects chosen by my son were exactly what were now on offer. This was even after all the other children had been in there first.

An amazing bonus was the opportunity to do music at school which had been denied him at his previous high school. Now his whole career and life is being outworked through a God-given ability to play and sing the most fantastic music. In fact he and his best friend Sam have just released their first music CD which is totally cool. Josh didn't have to lose a thing and he had everything he'd hoped for. ONE DOWN, FOUR TO GO.

Our second boy was due to start in the first year of high school. He was not really looking forward to this and especially now that he would have to start making completely new friends. I had quite a challenge on my hands to keep his morale up as well as negotiate with officials and the relevant staff that were handling his case. Again I was told that all the places were filled and it may take years to move him to our village school.

I really didn't want this for one moment and kept telling Daniel that I would not give up. I also kept challenging him to push through his feelings and to go to God for himself. If we're serious about living God's way then He will help us to bring our children with us and then we'll travel the faith journey together. We do this in an open and honest way which actually helps our kids relate with God, because when they see us in action they have something to follow. It's no surprise to them when we're not perfect, but they need to know how to reach for answers and we can show them if we dare.

This was a case of depending on God right in front of our child's beady eyes, even while it was his future at stake! I didn't think that I was to tackle it on my own but I sensed I had to step back a little and allow God to teach Daniel in the process.

> *'Train up a child in the way he should go [and in keeping with his individual gift or bent] and when he is old he will not depart from it.'* **Proverbs 22: 6**

I believe we should also encourage them as they grow to pray through issues of their own. Nothing was guaranteed, only my knowledge of a great God who embraces a challenge, and who loves our children as much as we do. I DIDN'T HAVE TO TRY TO MAKE GOD LOOK GOOD FOR MY SON'S SAKE, GOD CAN DO THAT FOR HIMSELF!

There was no news and I was asked to be patient and call again later. I then telephoned the school to check that Daniel's absence was ok for the first few days of term. I kept waiting until there was almost no time left and I found myself praying early one morning. God led me to read Psalms 115.

Most of the Psalm talks of His faithfulness to the house of Israel and of His faithfulness to the house of Aaron. So I prayed about it and confessed again concerning His faithfulness to the house of Owen!

As I finished praying, I looked down on that Friday morning and a phrase from the bottom of a magazine caught my eye. It read 'THE ANSWER COMES OUT OF THE BLUE'. About an hour later I was on the phone to a friend and we were talking about some other business. SHE USED EXACTLY THE SAME

PHRASE to tell me of another situation that she had just encountered. The answer for her had come out of the blue.

I KNEW INSTANTLY that Daniel's need was in the process of being met and I held on over the weekend. It was like hearing that still small voice all over again! I knew the struggle was over and dealt with and all I had to do was stand back and watch God ride through with our answer!

TO ME THIS PHRASE WAS CLEAR CONFIRMATION THAT IT WAS BREAKTHROUGH TIME. We had been learning at church about different peoples' ideas and perceptions of God. SOME PEOPLE BELIEVE IN GOD LIKE THIS!

FIRST THOUGHT.

God sits above the planet not noticing anyone, being quite happy to leave earth alone. Having his arms folded in quiet and content disassociation from the predicament below Him. Being preoccupied with His own comfort He doesn't notice that men and women scramble around to try and fix all the situations they find themselves in.

SECOND THOUGHT.

He leans over the banister of heaven to take a peek at the state of mankind with an affectionate glance. Here God the Father is standing at a safe distance. He is still motionless and definitely not engaging in any real ownership or responsibility for confused and lost humanity.

BEST THOUGHT. The one I know to be true.

He stoops down to lean over, with a longing for relationship in His heart. Now His arm outstretched and poised as if to unload countless blessings from his wide-open hand into our grateful arms. In this third posture He is clearly connecting with us. Knowing He has the answer in His grasp, He freely delivers the exact provision that we have need of.

These pictures reminded me of an Old Testament story:

> *'Then he said to me, 'Do not fear, Daniel, for from the first day that you set your heart to understand, and to humble yourself before your God, your words were heard; and I have come because of your words. But, the prince of the kingdom of Persia withstood me twenty-one days; and behold, Michael, one of the chief princes, came to help me, for I had been left alone there with the kings of Persia.'* **Daniel 10:12-13 (NKJV)**

The Daniel of the Bible had a problem and he always involved the right higher authority. HE PRAYED TO GOD! His answer took some time to arrive but he didn't give in to the pressure of delay or the pain of disappointment! Later he and an angel have a discussion over why it took so long for the answer to come.

On the first occasion that Daniel prayed fervently, God immediately sent and commissioned the angel to go and help. At the first call the angel set off on his rescue mission. Unbeknown to Daniel though, there were battles that the angel would have to win in order to reach him. The angel informed him that he had begun his journey to bring deliverance twenty-one days earlier. He'd been battling this way and that, until he'd finally made it through.

YOU MUST LISTEN TO THIS AND LEARN FROM IT!

All hope of recovery would have been lost during that time if this biblical Daniel had given up hope or changed his mind. He could have changed his prayer talk. He could have lost his focus and begun to try and sort it out for himself. He could have begun to doubt God's love and strength. If that had happened everything would have been different! The Lord would have had to send a huge whistle down the corridors of heaven to haul the angel back, and why? It would all be because Daniel couldn't keep praying and stay focused.

Sometimes the answer takes time to travel from the heavens to us, but we sure won't receive anything if we keep changing our mind. The double minded man or woman does not receive anything from the Lord, you can find it in the book of James.

> *'Only it must be in faith that he asks with no wavering (no hesitating, no doubting). For the one who wavers (hesitates, doubts) is like the billowing surge out at sea that is blown hither and thither and tossed by the wind. For truly, let not such a person imagine that he will receive anything [he asks for] from the Lord. [For being as he is] a man of two minds (hesitating, dubious, irresolute), [he is] unstable and unreliable and uncertain about everything [he thinks, feels, decides].'* **James 1:6-8**

God used this principle to teach me there and then. I had my comfort and rod (His word), to keep me on track for a few more days.

> *'He refreshes and restores my life (my self); He leads me in the paths of righteousness*

[uprightness and right standing with Him-
not for my earning it, but] for His name's
sake. Yes, though I walk through the [deep,
sunless] valley of the shadow of death, I
will fear or dread no evil, for You are with
me; Your rod [to protect] and Your staff [to
guide], they comfort me.'   **Psalm 23: 3-4**

Some of you have had to wait years for an
answer and you know what I'm talking about. I
pray right now for strength to your arm as you
reach high again for the undeniable favour and
blessing of God. Go for it and we will all cheer
together when you get your answer. I have been
caught by another truth that has transformed my
prayer life over the years.

'And this is the confidence (the assurance,
the privilege of boldness) which we have in
Him: [we are sure] that if we ask anything
(make any request) according to His will (in
agreement with His own plan), He listens to
and hears us. And if (since) we [positively]
know that He listens to us in whatever we
ask, we also know [with settled and
absolute knowledge] that we have [granted
us as our present possessions] the requests
made of Him.'   **1 John 5: 14-15**

You see if it's health you're after or salvation in
your house, then we have other scriptures that
categorically tell us what the will of the Lord is.
We cannot deny that He longs to see all men
saved. That's a done deal yet what we need now
is to appropriate wisdom to find out how we
can best bring the process to a good wholesome
conclusion.

Andrew's book called 'SENT' is an excellent
tool for those of us wishing to introduce others
to the Love and Saviour of our souls. It is filled
with excellent advice and pearls of wisdom. It

is inspirational and clear on the issues of soul winning and understanding evangelism. It can be used for personal growth or for the teaching of others!

Today's Christians recognise they need help and they are finding the 'HOW TO' of God's heart in excellent resource. There are lots of good books, tapes and CD's on the market that make our Christianity REAL and much more fun, more fruitful and more relevant.

Well, coming back to our own Daniel's school saga. Monday came and I was awake early to pray again and more importantly to seek God for the next step. I always telephoned in an enquiring and gentle fashion so that the battle I was facing was not transferred to the official at the other end of the phone. The last thing they needed was an irate mother on the end of the line!

People have no idea of how we struggle before God for the breakthrough and it is a good thing that they see us composed and certainly not aggressive toward them. Most of the time it would never work and it is usually quite inappropriate. On calling the school again during this Monday morning I was asked to wait and phone again later. I remember asking the school headmaster what the policy was concerning school places and telling him that I'd be praying that there'd be places for all the children that were waiting.

When I contacted the regional administration offices just minutes after, I was urged to make an appointment to visit a different neighbouring school. This was to check out another place for Daniel there so I asked for an appointment on Wednesday to give us two more days! He wouldn't have to start school there until

Thursday then. He really should have been settled into his new school by now and the pressure was on from the authorities.

That afternoon I was about to pray once more, when the Lord told me to go out and buy new school shoes for Daniel, as he'd need them for the following day! This was Monday and I KNEW IT WAS A DONE DEAL. GOD MADE ME TO KNOW IT IN MY HEART before anybody else had contacted me. I knew for sure that he would have his place in the village school, because he had to have his shoes for the following morning, and that was Tuesday. The appointment for the other school was not until Wednesday.

Within half an hour we were in the car on our way to the shops WHEN THE CALL CAME to give us the news we were expecting. Daniel had been given his place in our village school and was due to start the following day.

I thankfully cancelled our appointment with the other school, grateful to God that there had been no need to complicate the matter any further. Daniel knows for sure that the Lord stepped in on his behalf and saved him immense disruption. I DO REMIND HIM FROM TIME TO TIME.

TWO DOWN. Three to go!

A month after the boys were in to their new schools I was looking for a document, when I heard a voice tell me to go to the playgroup that morning. I knew it was due to close at 11.30am so I quickly gathered the little one and jumped into the car.

On arriving I was told that the playgroup was totally full for the whole year. I hadn't organised a place for him and wondered for a moment if I was too late. I somehow felt though that there must be a purpose for me having to be there right at that time on that specific day. As the playgroup leader spoke to me she said there was one place for a child to start in October and on finding that this was when Simeon would have his third birthday, THE PLACE WAS TO BE HIS.

We were both delighted to find things fitting into place and I knew God was on our case again. Simeon had so much fun there too, he just loved it.

TWO BOYS LEFT; LAST BUT NOT LEAST!

The two primary boys were placed temporarily into another local school and I continued to enquire about spaces in our village for them. This took a little longer, but they were quite happy to go with the flow, although I didn't want to see them settle and then have to uproot them all over again.

FAMILIES HAVE WAITED YEARS FOR PLACES. Many have given up in the process and eventually they've decided to keep their children in other schools to avoid any more disruption and pressure. So many times we were encouraged to wait and not expect too much. We were told that only one place may become available at first and we were given varied bits of advice as to whether to separate the boys or not. I really didn't want to separate them if possible.

One day I was wondering if I really was being too pushy in my prayer life and that maybe God was fed up of hearing my voice. Once before He'd told me to stop praying about a situation because he'd heard me and the answer was on its way! HE TOLD ME THAT THE OUTCOME WAS IN HAND and sure enough the breakthrough came for that situation soon after. In fact, I'm laughing right now because He's told me to quit praying about certain things at least twice in my lifetime. Both times He brought the resolve.

UNTIL YOU HEAR HIM SAY THAT, I SUGGEST YOU KEEP PRAYING.

On this occasion I went 'on my knees' again to see if maybe I should stop being so pre-occupied with our private life and focus on other things for a change? I wondered if I was taking the whole issue too far and becoming self-centred. I was still praying through a lot of other challenges as well though. It has become very clear to me that God teaches us in the field where we are at the time, for me over the years it was the home. For you it could be the workplace or the world of business.

> '...let us run with endurance the race that is set before us, looking unto Jesus, the author and finisher of our faith....'
> **Hebrews 12: 1-2 (NKJV)**

This means that he builds and then polishes us, just as a carpenter will construct a piece of furniture and then polish it until it shines. God Almighty made us and He's constantly and fondly improving us! In order to be able to continue with faith I needed a new word from God. When I asked God for this new revelation, He took me to the book of Hebrews:

> 'But the just shall live by faith [My righteous servant shall live by his conviction respecting man's relationship to God and divine things, and holy fervour born of faith and conjoined with it] ; and if

he draws back and shrinks in fear, My soul has no delight or pleasure in him.But our way is not that of those who draw back to eternal misery (perdition) and are utterly destroyed, but we are of those who believe [who cleave to and trust in and rely on God through Jesus Christ, the Messiah] and by faith preserve the soul.' **Hebrews 10: 38-39**

WE MUST NOT SHRINK BACK because there are huge consequences if we do. He'd not be pleased for one thing, and my answer would become a guaranteed negative so I guessed I'd been given the green light to carry on praying. It's good to get the green light to 'keep going', from God; it's then that you're given permission and strength to launch into another level of fight and faith.

A few weeks later I was on the phone to my dear friend who also needed a breakthrough for her children. Before I'd taken the call I'd opened the Bible to find another fresh word, (I see it as a sharp weapon in my hand which helps me to press forward and carve out a path for progress). It helps me in the way I think, talk and pray. It's the only way to get faith to come!

I long for and want answers and direction for life and it's always God's wisdom that brings these things. We all need Him so much and He loves to help us when we call on Him. It's no good relying on our own thought processes when we can have access to heavens computer base. After all we're taught that He came to give us life and life in all its fullness.

We need all He has for us so that we can serve Him in perfect health and peace. People will receive the best from us, if we're overflowing with the blessing of God. There is so much more to go around, and that is why He prospers His people. If all we want is to have just enough, we miss our opportunity to bless others. God gives us a testimony of breakthrough to lift someone else's faith. We are prospered financially not so that we can get rich and sit comfortably, but so that we can share it with others.

As my friend and I talked about the challenge we faced, a couple of thoughts went through my mind and I told her of them. It wasn't her fault but she was quite low about it all on this day and I began to dream a bit. I said that there could be someone on the phone to the headmistress right at that moment telling her that they had just sold their house and that they would be moving their children out from the school. We both knew that this could potentially open up the way for our children to be moved at last! It was a lovely thought!

We said goodbye after agreeing again to pray and not give up. I didn't have time to reach for my Bible before the phone rang again. I picked it up to hear the head mistress tell me that someone had just been on the line to inform her that they had just sold their house and that they would be moving their children out from the school.

The words that were spoken were exactly the same as mine! What's more, they had two children who were to each leave a space in the classes that my boys needed a place in. I WAS ECSTATIC and nearly climbed down the phone to hug the dear lady. I do hope she forgives me for squealing with delight in her delicate ear!

One of my favourite passages in the Bible is:

'When our sons shall be as plants grown large in their youth and our daughters as sculptured corner pillars hewn like those of a palace;' **Psalms 144: 12**

God delights in the strength and growth of our youth and He rescues them! The boys are yet young and I wait with anticipation for some of these prayers to be answered.

The story doesn't end there. I soon realised that being out of the village (and the city), meant that although I can drive I needed more help with transport. So, I began to pray for drivers to move into the village that we might be able to share the daily task of ferrying the family to all the different places we needed to be. Especially to school! Very soon after this I was visiting the school and a thoughtful and diligent secretary asked me to fill in a form because she thought we would be entitled to free school transport! Praise God we are, and since that time all of our boys have been taken by taxi to and from school everyday! The answer was there all along, but I wouldn't have known it unless someone had told me of it.

'Every intercessor has to learn to endure because he is dealing with what is invisible to the natural eye. The Holy Spirit will not tell us everything that is happening or give us the answer to all our questions, but He will show us all that we need to see and tell us all that we need to know for the strengthening of our faith and to enable us to hold on.'[11] **Arthur Wallis**

KEYS TO REMEMBER.

1. If God says move, then move anyway and believe for all the other needs to be met. You must know that He's told you to do it!

2. Give time for His answer and provision to come through, even when there is pressure to make a decision.

3. Once you know God has spoken stay on that word and pray it through unless He tells you otherwise. Learn to persevere even if the answer seems long in coming.

4. Don't try to work it out or change the way you pray because it will fog the whole process up. Allow God's creativity to shine through in the answers He brings.

5. Grow a good imagination and dare to speak it out loud. Use the words, 'wouldn't it be good if,' and 'just imagine if'.

6. Break the big picture down into smaller bits and deal with each need on its own merit.

9. I LOOK AFTER THEM

'Beware of paying attention or going back to what you once were, when God wants you to be something that you have never been.'[12]   **Oswald Chambers**

'But no weapon that is formed against you shall prosper, and every tongue that shall rise against you in judgement you shall show to be in the wrong. This [peace righteousness, security, triumph over opposition] is the heritage of the servants of the Lord [those in whom the ideal servant of the Lord is reproduced];this is the righteousness or the vindication which they obtain from me [this is that which I impart to them as their justification] says the Lord..'   **Isaiah 54:17**

Have you ever been threatened by a situation that was so completely out of your control that you knew you couldn't have handled it? Sometimes God sees to it perfectly so that you do not have to deal with it. In this instance He arranged for someone else to be right at the scene, someone who was more equipped and prepared for the dilemma at hand. The will of God is pleasing, perfect and acceptable.

'Do not be conformed to this world (this age), [fashioned after and adapted to its external, superficial customs], but be transformed (changed) by the [entire] renewal of your mind [by its new ideals and its new attitude], so that you may prove [for yourselves] what is the good and acceptable and perfect will of God, even the thing which is good and acceptable and perfect [in His sight for you].'   **Romans 12: 2**

That's the truth and it makes a huge difference to our outlook and expectation in all of life, if we see it this way. Not despite it all but actually in it all! It is a major privilege and blessed position that is stored up for the ones who literally live, eat and breathe the will of God.

> *'For the eyes of the Lord run to and fro throughout the whole earth, to show His might in behalf of those whose heart is blameless toward Him,'*
> **2 Chronicles 16: 9 (RSV)**

One day we were all working hard on a project in the house when my son ran in to tell of a crisis that had just occurred outside. I remember being physically shaken as he recounted the drama that had just unfolded in our garden that day. It seems OUR YOUNGEST SON WAS RUNNING AND PLAYING OUT ON THE LAWN. He was enjoying the freedom and bright sunshine on that clear day in March. He was three years old at the time.

Suddenly and without warning two massive ROTTWEILER DOGS ran into the garden and picked him up and tossed him around the garden LIKE A RAG DOLL! The dogs held him one on either side of his body by the sleeves of his jumper. They dragged him around the garden like this for a few minutes when my eldest son saw what was happening and ran outside to rescue his little brother.

I'd seen these dogs before and they were huge beasts to handle even for an adult. Most of the time they were under supervision, but this day they'd managed to break free. Their playful yet wild behaviour seemed so unpredictable.

I believe the Spirit of God must have arisen in Joshua's heart because he had the physical strength and emotional courage to literally kick the dogs away and carry Simeon into the house. Simeon did not have so much as a scratch on his body or a mark anywhere on his flesh. He carried on playing as if nothing had happened. I was speechless and in shock.

God knew for sure that this was not a battle that I was to fight. THANK GOD I WAS SPARED THIS NIGHTMARE because I couldn't imagine what I would have done if I'd been anywhere near the scene. If I'd stepped in, it would have been disastrous and God knew to keep me right out of the way on that occasion.

I couldn't speak of it for weeks and shuddered whenever I thought of it. It really bugged me and took away my courage for a while. Even so I knew I would get an answer and some comfort from somewhere, and it didn't stop me from pushing through to success with other things.

I needed something from the Lord that would bring peace and comfort, and God knew exactly what would do the trick! Whilst at a conference there was a question and answer time and a lady was asked about the welfare of her children and how she handled the thought of the amount of time that she was away from them. She was asked about the wellbeing of her children and the fact that she travelled so much. Her answer was from heaven as far as I was concerned, because she said that the Lord told her that He looked after them better than she did.

That was all I needed to equip me to face this memory and not let it unnerve me anymore. I prayed with grateful thanks and found a total release from the pressure it had tried to put me under. I found I could rise completely above this horrible assault and see God's smiling face as He assured me of His constant watch over our lives. His supernatural strength and power come through when we feel weak.

> *'Behold, He who keeps Israel will neither slumber nor sleep. The Lord is your keeper; the Lord is your shade on your right hand [the side not carrying a shield].The sun shall not smite you by day, nor the moon by night. The Lord will keep you from all evil; He will keep your life. The Lord will keep your going out and your coming in from this time forth and forevermore.'* **Psalms 121: 4-8**

The Bible says that He actually protects at all times, both in the day and in the night and that he guards our every move. To my absolute amazement Simeon happily plays with dogs and HE HAS NEVER HAD A NIGHTMARE OR A PROBLEM WITH FLASHBACKS. Only God could protect and heal in such an amazing way.

> *'The last of the human freedoms is to choose one's attitude in any given set of circumstances.'*[13]   **Victor Frankl (survivor of Nazi concentration camp)**

KEYS TO REMEMBER.

1. God's strength is made perfect in our weakness. Sometimes He just sends someone else when the situation is too tough.

   The Apostle Paul wrote of Jesus:

   > *'But He said to me, My grace (My favour and loving-kindness and mercy) is enough for you, (sufficient against any danger and enables you to bear the trouble manfully); for My strength and power are made perfect (fulfilled and completed) and show themselves most effective in (your) weakness. Therefore, I will all the more gladly glory in my weaknesses and infirmities, that the strength and power of Christ (the Messiah) may rest (yes, may pitch a tent over and dwell) upon me!'* **2 Corinthians 12:9**

2. God puts the right people in place to see that the gaps are covered when we're unable to deal with something.

3. As we continue to serve Him even with our unanswered questions He is ever mindful of our peace of mind and will send an answer somehow. The main thing is to trust Him in every situation.

4. God will show himself especially strong on behalf of those who desire to nurture and bring others through.

5. Don't think WOW look at the size of the problem! Think, 'Lord you always knew that between us we could handle that and get over it'!

10. THE DIAMONDS VISION

You may wonder how we can live for and serve God when all of these things have challenged us over the years. My view is this: how can we not live for and serve Him when He has so miraculously protected us through it all? There have been innumerable times when the sheer supernatural presence of Almighty God has swept in like a cloud.

HE IS BEAUTIFUL AND SO ARE HIS WORKS.

Our story is very small and insignificant alongside the things that other people have lived through. WE ARE HEALTHY, WE ARE CONNECTED, THE BOYS ARE WITH US IN EVERYTHING WE DO AND WE ARE RUNNING TOGETHER TO SET THE PACE THESE DAYS. IT'S A LIFESTYLE WORTH EVERY SECOND OF LIVING. I would sincerely choose no other way.

Over these many, adventurous years alongside Andrew, there have been countless people who have shared the journey with us. Some have helped and carried the load with us, many have also needed to be carried a part of the route, for seasons and stages along the way.

We have an awesome church of strong, gorgeous people who adore God and who love doing life together. You'll always find us in close proximity to what's going on with our church. There is something special for each one of us to do or get busy with. We're all fitting into the team and part of the building process together. JUST LIKE AN ENORMOUS FAMILY WITH LOTS OF MEMBERS WHO ARE ALL DIFFERENT BUT WHO ARE ALL

SO SPECIAL. WHENEVER SOMEONE IS MISSING THERE'S A GAP!

It's a wonderful experience to see lives and projects take shape, and carry influence and freedom into all sorts of places! For all of these years we've been a dynamic bunch of people growing in creativity and momentum to reach our destiny. On rare occasions we've stopped to rest just once in a while! We have grown up together with a deep desire to make God famous and bring together the lost souls who have not yet tapped into the purpose and reason for their lives.

My heart has always been that we would all play our part in this amazing building project and that everyone without exception would know that they're a valuable member of the building team. I believe that no task is unimportant or to be sniffed at, and that we should value others, ourselves and the varied responsibilities we are all required to carry. This would have a fantastic impact on our relationships and it would be hall-marked by the fact that we would all:

FIGHT IN FAITH TOGETHER, HIGHLIGHTED BY THE POWER OF SPEAKING THE TRUTH IN LOVE TO ONE ANOTHER. To achieve this we'd need to build relationships that are figuratively speaking: EYE TO EYE, HEART TO HEART, FACE TO FACE AND HAND IN HAND.

Eighteen years ago I wanted to share this message with a small group of women who had come to my house for a ladies' meeting. Bringing their tiny babies with them in travel seats, we had a great time. It was a treat to get some space for personal input.

As we prayed, I considered the message that was burning passionately in my heart and head. Just then there were three contributions that were brought as messages from God. They painted the perfect picture of my talk! It was amazing how God used three people to speak up and say something that helped to set the scene for the whole night.

What the first lady described was the picture of a jewel. It was a stunningly unique and priceless gem. Cut and beautifully shaped to reflect the light around. It was a gem on its own, quite gorgeous but isolated.

The next contribution was about a collection of different jewels that were still different and quite wonderful but now they reflected light in one another, because they were formed into a necklace. Not losing their individuality but shining together and appearing quite spectacular. Connected and joined on either side with links that were positioned there to strategically hold them in relationship.

The final image was of a crown fitted with bedazzling jewels that were not only connected but firmly set in place. Each unique gem was in its own specific setting to form a picture not just of beauty but of authority, positioning and influence. In the book of Isaiah we read:

'For Zion's sake I will not hold My peace, And for Jerusalem's sake I will not rest, Until her righteousness goes forth as brightness, And her salvation as a lamp that burns. The Gentiles shall see your righteousness, And all kings your glory. You shall be called by a new name, Which the mouth of the Lord will name. You shall also be a crown of glory In the hand of the Lord, And a royal diadem In the hand of your

*God. You shall no longer be termed
Forsaken, Nor shall your land any more be
termed Desolate; But you shall be called
Hephzibah, and your land Beulah; For the
Lord delights in you, And your land shall be
married. For as a young man marries a
virgin, So shall your sons marry you; And
as the bridegroom rejoices over the bride,
So shall your God rejoice over you.'*

Isaiah 62:1-5 (NKJV)

Over these many years those words and
relationships have been tested considerably and
many of the original women whose children
have long since outgrown those tiny car seats
are thankfully still with me. Not one ounce of
fervour for God has been lost; in fact their very
lives are given over to the nurturing and
equipping of others.

Authority and influence are carried into many of
life's arenas as women are finding their skills
magnified and released for others to benefit
from. They teach, train and inspire others to
shake off the past and expect more from our
loving heavenly Father. Their gifts, talents and
acquired knowledge are carefully polished to
impact the lives of those they meet. All women
who are works in progress have the potential to
accurately reflect the dynamics of a salvation
that keeps transforming them and the people in
their world.

At last we're seeing the release of these skills of
counselling, loving, caring and administration.
Abilities that are free to function can and do
transform many lives.

GIFTS OF HOSPITALITY, MUSICIANSHIP,
LEADERSHIP, CREATIVITY AND
BUSINESS ARE EMERGING FROM UNDER
THE LAUNDRY BASKET AND THE

OFFICE SCHEDULE. Potential that we only dreamed about is being released and it is now finding space to flourish and literally change the shape of our horizons. The best in them is developed and invested into society, to bring through the hidden treasure in others.

As women STUDY the word of God from other ministries and their own personal reading, they begin to stand up. They STAND UP firstly on the inside in their self-esteem and their sense of belonging and value. They then can truly learn to stand up on the outside and carry influence with a clear and confident voice.

Once this transformation has taken place there'll be the opportunity to SPEAK UP. To speak up with a voice that is loud and clear with wisdom and passion that cannot be ignored. Women don't have to wait for an invitation to a platform in order to speak. Everyday there are countless opportunities at the school gate, in the office, waiting in the grocery queue to share how much Jesus means to us.

We are to be living lives of worship and honour before the most wonderful Saviour, but we must remember the world is watching. It's a fact that God looks at the heart but the people around us cannot see our heart at first. They look at how we take care of ourselves and those around us. They look at our dress sense, attention to detail and wellbeing. So when everything else is in place there must be a good and bright way to SPARKLE and get noticed in a godly and unselfish way that gives Him the Glory and makes Him famous.

> '... For the Lord sees not as man sees; for man looks on the outward appearance, but the Lord looks at the heart.'
> **1 Samuel 16: 7**

Diamonds is a vision that's about releasing and enlarging human capabilities and has life-changing potential for anyone that can and will catch it.

'For we walk by faith, not by sight.'
2 Corinthians 5:7 (RSV)

To change lives one by one is a goal that's attainable and possible, when we walk in this way. WE'RE CONNECTING TO CONQUER those things that need to change and be put right on the planet and in each individual life.

We have to reach into the resource of heaven to see miracles happen and actually have faith for someone else's growth, development and success. BELIEVING IN THEM AND KNOWING THAT GOD HAS FAITH FOR THEM. The day is coming when we will see changes in cities and even nations, as people respond to His voice.

In the book of Isaiah God says:

'See, I have inscribed you on the palms of my hands; Your walls are continually before Me.'
Isaiah 49:16

King David prayed:

'Keep me as the apple of your eye; hide me in the shadow of your wings.'
Psalms 17: 8 NIV

In fact I get the impression that God can't get enough of us. He wants us to be as close as possible. This relationship is here for the building and it's the safest, sweetest most wonderful place to be. As a teenager when I was a new Christian I cried as I pondered over God's choosing of me. Feeling totally worthless and not much use to Him I offered myself up. Then God showed me a scripture that gave me some meaning.

'For [simply] consider your own call, brethren; not many [of you were considered to be] wise according to human estimates and standards, not many influential and powerful, not many of high and noble birth. [No] for God selected (deliberately chose) what in the world is foolish to put the wise to shame, and what the world calls weak to put the strong to shame. And God also selected (deliberately chose) what in the world is lowborn and insignificant and branded and treated with contempt, even the things that are nothing, that He might depose and bring to nothing the things that are, So that no mortal man should[(have pretense for glorying and] boast in the presence of God. But it is from Him that you have your life in Christ Jesus, Whom God made our Wisdom from God,[(revealed to us a knowledge of the divine plan of salvation previously hidden, manifesting itself as] our righteousness [thus making us upright and putting us in right standing with God], and our Consecration [making us pure and holy], and our Redemption [providing our ransom from eternal penalty for sin]. So then, as it is written, Let him who boasts and proudly rejoices and glories, boast and proudly rejoice and glory in the Lord.' **1 Corinthians 1:26-31**

I saw myself in there and I knew that He was speaking of me. I knew I was not wise or noble or strong in any way. He then led me to read another part of the Bible in which I understood a simple but necessary challenge which was to walk closely by His side and keep His word in my head and heart. If I would live it then He would bless me. I also read:

'No man shall be able to stand before you all the days of your life; as I was with Moses, so I will be with you; I will not fail you or forsake you. Be strong and of good courage; for you shall cause this people to inherit the land which I swore to their fathers to give them. Only be strong and very courageous, being careful to do according to all the law which Moses my servant commanded you; turn not from it to the right hand or the left, that you may have good success wherever you go. This book of the law shall not depart out of your mouth, but you shall meditate on it day and night, that you may be careful to do according to all that is written in it; for then you shall make your way prosperous and then you shall have good success. Have I not commanded you? Be strong and of good courage; be not frightened, neither be dismayed; for the Lord your God is with you wherever you go.' **Joshua 1: 5-9 RSV**

He finally took me back to Corinthians:

'What eye has not seen and ear has not heard, and has not entered into the heart of man, [all that] God has prepared (made and keeps ready) for those who love Him [who hold Him in affectionate reverence, promptly obeying Him and gratefully recognising the benefits he has bestowed]. Yet to us God has unveiled and revealed them by and through His Spirit, for the [Holy] Spirit searches diligently, exploring and examining everything, even sounding the profound and bottomless things, of God [the divine counsels and things hidden and beyond man's scrutiny].' **1 Corinthians 2:9**

I believe that this is the day, and we will see an awesome move of God in our generation as people dare to believe that there is a Holy Spirit and also as they learn to listen carefully to His intimate instruction.

It will happen as we work this out with our families and friends alongside, with relationships that are strong and healthy. To NEGOTIATE DECISIONS WELL, and to LEAP OVER the obstacles and begin to SOAR ABOVE the mundane IS OUR DESTINY.

We as the church are to be a light shining in a dark world. Relevant for our day and packaged carefully so that the eyes of the world gaze upon us and remain here until she decides to come and taste for herself. In His presence awesome exchanges take place. I bring my worship and He gives me healing, I offer my life and He brings benefits that I cannot contain so that they spill over and resource my neighbour. As individuals and as a huge crowd we can get good at hearing Him and finding His light in the darkness.

CONCLUSION

So there you have just some of the adventures that we have seen as we've travelled so far. Some I would not have chosen, but in His grace we've come through them all, able to sing more clearly than ever of a God who loves us, and who has never abandoned us!

It may be that you are not sure if He's there for you, because you've never asked Him to be, or you think that your link with him is not secure enough to dare to test it out. As a teenager I asked Him to be my Saviour and my Lord even though I didn't know all of what it would entail. I KNEW THEN THAT THERE WAS A GAP in my life and I was told that only God could fill it. I wondered if God could possibly understand the needs of individuals in this day and age.

Would His answers be relevant for my life? Life is a journey and we often need help in order to negotiate the good and the bad with wisdom and strength. I know that I could have been a loser on so many occasions and only my connection with Him has saved the day and the situation. I am so grateful that someone told me about Him when they did!

Please let me help you for a moment. It's quite simply a choice of coming straight with God and asking Him to be there. He's busy you know, but if He hears you call you can be assured He'll stop to listen.

Here are some verses that make things clear:

'Since all have sinned and are falling short of the honour and glory which God bestows and receives.' **Romans 3:23**

We soon have to realise that we don't match up to God's standards. We can only be made right by faith, not by our own hard work:

'For we hold that a man is justified and made upright by faith independent of and distinctly apart from good deeds (works of the Law). [The observance of the Law has nothing to do with justification.]' **Romans 3:28**

Jesus is waiting for you to tell Him that you need Him and the truth is we all need Him. We cannot ignore the proof:

'[All] are justified and made upright and in right standing with God, freely and gratuitously by His grace (His unmerited favour and mercy), through the redemption which is [provided] in Christ Jesus.' **Romans 3: 24**

After your relationship with God has been put right there is another step to take, this is only the beginning! You have to tell Him that you'll go His way through the roundabouts of life. God really wants a relationship and doesn't just want to catch up with you in heaven. Even if you struggle to say it, be assured of your need to decide, and then say it anyway. He'll take you through each turn as it arrives, and of course only one at a time or you'll have a collision!

GOD IS VERY STEADY AND TRUE, AND HIS LOVE WILL STEER AND COMFORT YOU AS YOU GO.

You'll need to tell someone that you prayed like this, and that you asked Him to forgive you and to give you a new start, asking Jesus to be your Lord, and Saviour. He must become your Lord because you need Him to take charge. When you had the steering wheel things were a bit tricky and you were vulnerable to say the least. You need Him to become your Saviour because He really and truthfully rescues ALL WHO CALL UPON HIS NAME. There is no other name by which a man must be saved but by the name of Jesus.

> *'And there is salvation in and through no one else, for there is no other name under heaven given among men by and in which we must be saved.'* **Acts 4: 12**

> *'And it shall be that whoever shall call upon the name of the Lord [invoking, adoring, and worshiping the Lord-Christ] shall be saved.'* **Acts 2:21**

Please don't think that it will be a case of praying it once only and thinking that that is enough. You will be fit for heaven and your salvation will be fixed securely, but there is all of life to be worked through. You'll find that you will have to keep going back to Him to reaffirm your decision. This is because it's too easy to take the steering wheel back when you get a little confidence or happiness, or even worry. Also if things don't go the way you planned you may panic and try to take control again for yourself.

Next, you need to find people who you can share the journey with. It's so much better to do life together with Christians who love God, and live good lives. Just being with us will encourage you to stay on track, at a good and steady pace. There is so much life ready for you to live. He has lavishly prepared it all for you!

Do you know there is a place for everyone in God's house only some people just never make it a priority to be involved? The family is already gathered and the party has kicked into gear. We miss you if you're not around, you leave a space that no-one else can fill!

He is not here on the earth right now, but neither has he left us alone to muddle through. Jesus has sent His partner the Holy Spirit, who is the one that whispers all these wonderful and amazing gems into your ear. He lovingly wants to protect, lead and inspire people. To take them on to a better existence and lifestyle even in the humdrum and sometimes critical stages that are faced.

Find Him too and ask to be baptised in the Holy Spirit. Receive His special power to be more than victorious in your life. Jesus sent him for that very purpose and you miss out on a lovely and powerful friendship if you don't know the guidance of the Holy Spirit in your daily life.

Did you know that both Jesus and the Holy Spirit pray for you to succeed and to grow in strength?

'So too the [Holy] Spirit comes to our aid and bears us up in our weakness; for we do not know what prayer to offer nor how to offer it worthily as we ought, but the Spirit Himself goes to meet our supplication and pleads in our behalf with unspeakable yearnings and groanings too deep for utterance. And He who searches the hearts of men knows what is in the mind of the [Holy] Spirit [what His intent is], because the Spirit intercedes and pleads [before

*God] in behalf of the saints according to
and in harmony with God's will.'*
Romans 8:26-27

*'Therefore He (Jesus) is able also to save to
the uttermost (completely, perfectly, finally,
and for all time and eternity) those who
come to God through Him, since He is
always living to make petition to God and
intercede with Him and intervene for them.'*
Hebrews 7:25

Becoming a Christian and partnering with
others will change the course of your life and
possibly that of your family too! Come and
introduce yourself you're welcome to call in
and visit anytime. Come and see. God is more
precious than any treasure, but as surely as a
diamond sparkles He is worth searching for. So,
if you're still wondering; is God there? YOU
BET!

I AM

I will be your light in the darkness,
I will hold your tears as they fall.
I will turn your night into day time.
Hold on - hold on.

I will bring you faith when you falter,
I will give you strength for the storm.
I will make you smile in the morning.
Hold on - hold on.

You need to know that I am here
Each time you call me;
You need to see my love
In everything I've made.
Do you believe that I can catch
The faintest whisper?
Just remember this -
That I count every breath you take.

Hold on, I am here for you.
Hold on, my love will see you through.
I am the answer when you ask,
I'll be your partner as you dance.
Hold on ………..

Lyrics by Sue Owen

Bibliography

[1] Maxwell, John C, (2001) *The Power of Attitude*, River Oak Publishing

[2] Lombardi, Vince, in *The Power of Attitude* (2001), River Oak Publishing

[3] Einstein, Albert, in *The Power of Attitude* (2001), River Oak Publishing

[4] Watts, Isaac, 1674-1748, Hymn-writer

[5] Chambers, Oswald, (1995) *My Utmost for His Highest,* Oswald Chambers Publications Association

[6] Ibid

[7] Wallis, Arthur, (1995) *Pray in the Spirit,* Kingsway Communications

[8] Ibid

[9] Engstrom, Ted W, (1982) *The Pursuit of Excellence,* Zondervan Publishing

[10] Marguleas, Howard, in *The Leader in You, (1995),* Dale Carnegie, Simon & Schuster Inc

[11] Wallis, Arthur, (1995) *Pray in the Spirit,* Kingsway Communications

[12] Chambers, Oswald, (1995) *My Utmost for His Highest,* Oswald Chambers Publications Association

[13] Frankl, V. (1985) *Man's Search for Meaning,* New York, Basic Books